Managing Currency Options in Financial Institutions

T0295708

This book presents practices for managing currency options with the Vanna-Volga method. It describes the underlying theories and applications of the Vanna-Volga method in managing currency options of a financial institution while conforming to the Basel III regulatory requirements, which demand a high consistency between the valuation and market risk calculation methodologies of financial instruments.

The book includes technical details that shed understanding on the major applications, including valuation, volatility recovery, dynamic portfolio replication and value-at-risk. Those who study finance, risk management, quantitative finance or similar areas, as well as practitioners who wish to learn how to valuate, hedge and manage the market risk of currency options with more advanced models and techniques, will find the book of invaluable use.

Yat-fai LAM is the Principal at Structured Products Analytics of CapitaLogic Limited, an adjunct faculty teaching master programmes in banking/finance/financial engineering/financial services at City University of Hong Kong and an adjunct dissertation supervisor of The University of Warwick's Master of Science programmes in Hong Kong. Prior to assuming his current positions, Yat-fai has worked for a bank regulator, an international bank, an asset management firm and a credit rating agency, specializing in the implementation of the Basel New Capital Accord.

Kin-keung LAI received his PhD at Michigan State University in 1977 and is currently a Chair Professor of Management Science at the City University of Hong Kong. He is the president of the Asia-Pacific Industrial Engineering and Management Society, the General Secretary of the Hong Kong Operational Research Society and a council member of the International Federation of Operations Research Societies. His main research interests include supply chain and operation management, forecasting, computational intelligence and risk analysis.

Routledge Advances in Risk Management
Edited by Kin-keung LAI and Shouyang Wang

Managing Currency Options in Financial Institutions

Vanna-Volga method

Yat-fai LAM and Kin-keung LAI

LONDON AND NEW YORK

First published 2016 by Routledge

2 Park Square, Milton Park, Abingdon, Oxfordshire OX14 4RN
711 Third Avenue, New York, NY 10017

Routledge is an imprint of the Taylor & Francis Group, an informa business

First issued in paperback 2018

British Library Cataloguing-in-Publication Data

A catalogue record for this book is available from the British Library

Library of Congress Cataloging-in-Publication Data
Lam, Yat-Fai.
   Managing currency options in financial institutions : Vanna-Volga method / Yat-Fai Lam and Kin-Keung Lai.
      pages cm. — (Routledge advances in risk management)
   1. Options (Finance)   2. Foreign exchange futures.   3. Currency swaps.   4. Bank investments.   5. Financial risk management.
I. Lai, Kin Keung.   II. Title.
   HG6024.A3L3266 2015
      332.4'5—dc23   2015011524

ISBN: 978-1-138-77805-4 (hbk)
ISBN: 978-1-138-31693-5 (pbk)

Typeset in Times
by Apex CoVantage, LLC

Contents

Figures

Tables

About the authors

Dr. Yat-fai LAM

Dr. Yat-fai LAM is an Adjunct Assistant Professor of Finance at The University of Hong Kong, the MSc Dissertation Supervisor of the postgraduate programmes conducted in Hong Kong by The University of Warwick and the Adjunct Faculty of Finance at City University of Hong Kong. Dr. LAM has worked for a bank regulator, an international bank, an asset management firm, a financial advisory firm and a credit rating agency, specializing in structured products, credit risk management and the Basel III framework.

Dr. LAM graduated from the City University of Hong Kong with a Doctor of Business Administration (Finance) degree. He holds the CFA, CAIA, FRM and PRM designations issued by the CFA Institute, CAIA Association, GARP and PRMIA, respectively. Also, Dr. LAM was honored with the "PRM Award of Merit 2005" by PRMIA for his outstanding results in the PRM examination.

Prof. Kin-keung LAI

Prof. Kin-keung LAI received his PhD at Michigan State University. He is currently the Chair Professor of Management Science at the City University of Hong Kong. Prior to his current post, he was a Senior Operational Research Analyst for Cathay Pacific Airways and an Area Manager of Marketing Information Systems for Union Carbide Eastern. Professor Lai's main areas of research interests are operations and supply chain management, financial and business risk analysis and modelling using computational intelligence. He has published extensively in international refereed journals on the above areas.

In 2009, Professor LAI received the Joon S. Moon Distinguished International Alumni Award of the Michigan State University and also was appointed as the Chang Jiang Scholar Chair Professor by the Ministry of Education, China. In 2012, he was ranked fourth among academic authors in the area of Business Intelligence and Analytics worldwide in the MIS Quarterly Special Issue. In 2014, he was the recipient of the Civil and Environmental Engineering Distinguished Alumni Award from Michigan State University.

Preface

This book examines the application of the Vanna-Volga method in managing currency options for financial institutions according to the Basel III regulatory requirements, which demand a high consistency between the currency option valuation and market risk measurement methodologies for financial instruments.

The book extends the application of Vanna-Volga method from currency option valuation to value-at-risk ("VaR") amount calculation and dynamic portfolio replication. The accuracy of currency option valuation is assessed with the variation between the volatility smiles derived by the Vanna-Volga method and those implied by the market prices of traded currency options. The efficiency of VaR amount calculation is verified by the back testing results of one-day VaR amount at the 99th percentile confidence level. The effectiveness of dynamic portfolio replication is measured by the discrepancy between the value of the dynamic replicating portfolio and the currency option's payoff at maturity.

The empirical results in this book demonstrates that the Vanna-Volga option valuation framework, while providing an effective valuation correction to the classical Black-Scholes model, is also a practical and affordable approach for VaR amount calculation and dynamic portfolio replication. The relevant computations can be derived with data readily available from major financial information providers and in closed form solutions. These advantages are less observable in other advanced option valuation frameworks.

Yat-fai LAM
City University of Hong Kong

Kin-keung LAI
City University of Hong Kong

1 Introduction

This chapter introduces the basics of currency options and the initiative of the Vanna-Volga method.

1.1 Background

Currency options are among the most actively traded financial instruments in the world (BIS, 2012). Banks and insurance companies utilize currency options to hedge their currency exposures against the potential loss arising from the fluctuation of currency rates. Hedge funds use currency options to speculate on the direction of currency rates and volatility movements in order to maximize profit with minimum initial cash outflows.

The option market was essentially boosted by the seminal work by Black and Scholes (1973) and Merton (1973), who proposed the first option valuation framework, which facilitated Scholes and Merton's winning the Nobel Prize in economics in 1997.[1] This option valuation framework, indeed, opened a new branch of research in finance study.

For a financial institution participating in currency option trading, the major trading activities include (DeRosa, 2011), among others:

- Acquiring a currency option and exercising the currency option if it registers a positive payoff at maturity, i.e. the currency option is in-the-money (ITM);
- Writing a currency option and delivering the underlying currency when the currency option is ITM at maturity;
- Acquiring a currency option and entering an offsetting transaction some times later before maturity to lock in the unrealized profit or stop loss; and
- Writing a currency option and entering an offsetting transaction some times later before maturity in order to lock in the unrealized profit or stop loss.

1.2 Management of currency options

In addition, once a currency option transaction has been entered into the ledger of a financial institution, the financial institution needs to manage the currency option by performing three major tasks:

- Option valuation: calculate the theoretical value of a currency option in order to estimate the unrealized profit and loss on periodic basis. This is accomplished by some currency option valuation models;
- Risk measurement: calculate the market risk of a currency option in order to assess whether the risk is in line with the risk appetite of the financial institution. In accordance with international banking practices, market risk is measured by the one-day value-at-risk (VaR) amount at the 99th percentile confidence level (BCBS, 2009);
- Dynamic hedging: eliminate the price fluctuation of a currency option by entering an offsetting portfolio with the same risk sensitivity in order to lock in the unrealized profit and loss in case it is inappropriate to enter an identical offsetting currency option transaction for some reason (e.g. the currency option market is lacking counterparties or the identical offsetting currency option is too expensive). The process of dynamic hedging is identical to the construction and continuous adjustment of a dynamic replicating portfolio until maturity. This dynamic replicating portfolio has the same risk sensitivity as the currency option and consists of the underlying currency, domestic cash and other related liquidly traded financial instruments. For a long position in currency option, dynamic hedging is performed by entering into a short position of the dynamic replicating portfolio. In contrast, for a short position in a currency option, dynamic hedging is performed by entering into a long position of the dynamic replicating portfolio. This dynamic replicating portfolio is rebalanced frequently to match the continually changing value and risk sensitivity of the currency option until maturity.

Since currency options are highly customized contracts and traded over the counter (OTC), market prices of the majority of transacted currency options are not communicated to practitioners through financial information providers. Only the implied volatilities of currency options at standard maturities and standard moneynesses are exhibited. As such, financial institutions take an indirect approach, using quantitative models with limited publicly available key data from financial information providers to valuate currency options. These quantitative models are also utilized to calculate the one-day VaR amounts and to construct the dynamic replicating portfolio.

The Black-Scholes model is by far the most popular currency option valuation model utilized by practitioners in the currency option market for option valuation, VaR amount calculation and dynamic portfolio replication, primarily because of the model's simplicity and highly analytical tractability. Nevertheless, the Black-Scholes model is also criticized for its oversimplified assumptions of an underlying stochastic process of currency rates in simple geometric Brownian motion. Empirically, this oversimplified treatment results in a nonconstant implied volatility that contradicts the initial model assumption of single constant volatility (Wystup, 2008).

Academics addressed this issue from the fundamental assumptions of an underlying stochastic process of currency rate and derived a number of advanced option valuation models, including, among others, Heston's (1993) stochastic volatility model, Duan's (1995) GARCH option model and Madan, Carr and Chang's (1998) Variance Gamma model.

These advanced option models are very successful in characterizing the dynamics of currency options on a theoretically sound basis. Nevertheless, these advanced option models lack the ability to express the option value in closed-form solutions with data directly obtainable from major financial information providers. These two limitations restrict the applicability of those advanced option models. The calibration requirements and numerical methods demand high computing power, which makes them difficult to put into practice when the advanced option models are extended to the areas of VaR amount calculation and dynamic portfolio replication, particularly for financial institutions with a large number of currency options in their portfolios. Financial institutions may thus be forced to use one model for valuating currency options, one model for calculating one-day VaR amounts and one model for constructing dynamic replicating portfolios. This works against the principle set out by the Basel Committee on Bank Supervision (2009), which demands a high consistency in using option valuation models to manage currency options.

Practitioners, on the other hand, demand a model with simplicity and analytical tractability compatible with those of the Black-Scholes model. Moreover, the large number of products and services already developed around the Black-Scholes model make the model very convenient when the Black-Scholes model is applied to option valuation, VaR amount calculation and dynamic portfolio replication. As such, practitioners seek to improve the Black-Scholes model through their practical experiences with some less rigorous arguments. This results in the 'trader's rule of thumb' (TROT), which aims at improving the Black-Scholes model by using the market prices of three liquidly traded currency options

Nevertheless, the lack of rigorous underlying theory restricts the application of the TROT within the scope of currency option valuation. More important, Wystup (2008) showed that when the parameters of any one of the three liquidly traded currency options are substituted in the TROT formulas, the TROT formulas fail to produce currency option values that are equal to the market prices of the three liquidly traded currency options. This result demonstrates a critical internal inconsistency within the TROT framework.

1.3 Currency option valuation

Financial institutions essentially need a theoretically sound, empirically accurate and readily implemented option valuation model to serve as the basis on which to manage their currency options. Theoretical soundness facilitates the extension of an option valuation model from the sole application of currency option valuation to VaR amount calculation and dynamic portfolio replication in a uniform manner. Empirical accuracy ensures that a currency option valuation model produces figures that have sufficient precision to aid in decision making. Convenience of implementation allows the adaption of the option valuation model with affordable resources.

Recognizing the theoretical limitation of a pure practitioners' approach to constructing the TROT, Castagna and Mercurio (2007) derived the theory of the Vanna-Volga method by revamping the TROT on a more solid theoretical foundation and demonstrated that with the hedging by three liquidly traded currency options, an improvement to the TROT, namely the Vanna-Volga method, could be utilized to derive a complete volatility smile with very few input parameters. This volatility smile is compatible with the volatility smile implied by the market prices of the currency options. A more rigorous justification for the Vanna-Volga method was provided by Shkolnikov (2009), and the application to exotic currency options was described by Bosens, Rayée, Skantzos and Deelstra (2010). The theory suggests that, with some fundamental improvements supported by a moderate level of mathematics, there is a strong potential to apply the Vanna-Volga method in other practical applications in relation to the management of currency options.

Nevertheless, so far, no study has evaluated a rigorous model validation process to ascertain the overall accuracy of the Vanna-Volga method in valuating currency options. Moreover, the theories of the application of the Vanna-Volga method to VaR amount calculation and dynamic portfolio replication have not been adequately studied. Apparently, there is a need to fill these gaps in the literature before the Vanna-Volga method can be seriously considered as a feasible model for managing currency options in financial institutions.

1.4 Importance of currency option valuation

According to statistics from the Bank for International Settlement (2011), as of June 2011, the outstanding volume of currency options traded OTC amounted to US$ 11,358 bn. Moreover, another survey from the Bank for International Settlements (2010) also suggested that the average global daily turnover of currency options increased to US$ 207 bn in 2010 from US$ 87 bn, an increase of 238 percent over a period of 12 years.

In addition, the Foreign Exchange Committee (2011) reported in its Survey of North American Foreign Exchange Volume that the average daily volume of currency options (after adjustment for double counting of transactions between members) of 25 major financial institutions amounted to US$ 32 bn, an increase of 21 percent over the previous year.

These surveys all exhibited the materiality of currency options in the global financial market and their impacts on financial institutions' profit and loss and market risk exposures. A small deficiency in a currency option management framework may be amplified by the huge volume of transactions, resulting in large problems.

Essentially, these huge figures all reconfirm the need for a theoretically sound, empirically accurate and readily implemented currency option management framework.

1.5 Book objective

This book records and summarizes the authors' study aimed at assessing whether the Vanna-Volga method is a feasible method for managing currency options in financial institutions. This objective is accomplished in both the theoretical and the empirical dimensions.

Along the theoretical dimension, the theory of the Vanna-Volga method is developed, extended and enriched to the areas of VaR amount calculation and dynamic portfolio replication. These include the derivation of the one-day VaR amount formulas and dynamic portfolio replication process under the Vanna-Volga method.

Along the empirical dimension, the theories on currency option valuation, VaR amount calculation and dynamic portfolio replication are validated against some well-established references.

It is expected that the results from the Vanna-Volga method will constitute a significant improvement to the Black-Scholes model. The close relationship between the Vanna-Volga method and the Black-Scholes model ensures that most industry services currently available to financial institutions will also be applicable to the Vanna-Volga method.

1.6 Questions

The main goal of this book is to answer the following master question: is the Vanna-Volga method a superior approach for managing current options in financial institutions over the Black-Scholes model?

The superiority of the Vanna-Volga method is essentially assessed by the following questions:

- Is the Vanna-Volga method an accurate approach to valuate currency options? At first glance, this question may be answered by a naïve approach that calculates the value of a liquidly traded currency option and compares the calculated option value with the price observed from the market. Nevertheless, the values of currency option may be affected by their sensitivity to volatility. While the value of a deeply ITM currency option is insensitive to volatility, the value of a deeply OTM currency option is extremely sensitive to volatility. Therefore, some academics choose to perform accuracy test on option valuation models in alternative ways, according to Beneder and Elkenbrcht-Huizing (2003).

  To eliminate the effects of other dependent variables, the accuracy of an option valuation method is assessed, for the same currency option, by comparing two implied volatilities, one from the option valuation model and one from the market prices. Since the Black-Scholes formulas directly define the relationship between currency option value and implied volatility, given that (i) the market rate of currency and risk-free rates are observable, and (ii) the strike rate and maturity are specified in a currency option contract, for a given currency option value, either calculated with the Vanna-Volga method or observed from the market price, the corresponding implied volatility is uniquely defined. Thus a comparison is made by following these steps: (i) calculate the value of a liquidly traded currency option with the Vanna-Volga method and back out an implied volatility with Black-Scholes formulas; (ii) observe the market price of this liquidly traded currency option and back out an implied volatility with Black-Scholes formulas; (iii) assess how close these two implied volatilities are. A collection of implied volatilities among a group of currency options with same maturity but different moneyness provides a comparison of two implied volatility smiles, one from the model values and one from market prices. It is expected that an accurate currency option valuation method will produce a volatility smile that is close to the volatility smile derived from the market prices.

- How robust is the Vanna-Volga method in recovering a volatility smile? According to the theory, the Vanna-Volga method is able to recover the entire volatility smile from the market prices of only three liquidly traded currency options, usually with an ATM option at the middle and two wing currency options on two sides of the volatility smile. A higher accuracy is expected for the implied volatilities between the wing currency options. Nevertheless, a robust volatility recovery method is expected also to produce sufficiently accurate volatilities at both ends of the volatility smile outside two wing currency options.

- Is the volatility smile derived from the Vanna-Volga method efficient in calculating the one-day VaR amount? Under the Vanna-Volga method, both the market rate of underlying currency and implied volatility are major risk factors. These market risk factors are inserted into a one-day VaR amount formula for currency options in order to arrive at the one-day VaR amounts. These one-day VaR amounts are further back tested in accordance with the Basel II framework on market risk. It is expected that an efficient one-day VaR amount formula will register around 1 percent of violations on average.

- Is the Vanna-Volga method effective in performing dynamic portfolio replication? In order to construct a dynamic replicating portfolio, the amounts of liquidly trade financial instruments, that is the hedging ratios, are calculated by the option valuation model. If this replicating portfolio is rebalanced frequently, for example on daily basis, to match the value of the currency option until maturity, it is expected that the dynamic replicating portfolio at maturity will be close to the final payoff of the currency option.

1.7 Deliverables

A number of outcomes from the study are presented to address the study questions set out in section 1.6. Specifically, the study produced the following deliverables to facilitate the assessment of the Vanna-Volga method.

On the theoretical side, the mathematical framework of the Vanna-Volga method is enriched to derive formulas that facilitate the calculations of hedging ratios for the dynamic replicating portfolio. On the basis of the hedging ratios, a one-day VaR amount formula for currency options is developed. In addition, the practical process for dynamic portfolio replication is deduced.

On the empirical side, a statistical analysis is performed to assess the accuracy of the volatility smile recovered by the Vanna-Volga method against that implied by the market prices of currency options. An additional assessment is conducted with a focus on both ends of the volatility smile to ascertain whether the Vanna-Volga method is sufficiently robust. Furthermore, a back testing on the one-day VaR amount formula in accordance with the Basel II market risk framework is conducted to assess whether the Vanna-Volga method will produce an efficient estimate of market risk. Another analysis is performed to compare the dynamic replication performance of the Vanna-Volga method and the Black-Scholes model.

For the test on volatility recovery, an identical set of statistical analysis is also performed, using the Malz formula as a baseline case. This facilitates a comparative analysis between the Vanna-Volga method and the existing practices to discover how much model improvement would be introduced by using the Vanna-Volga method.

1.8 Contributions

This study contributes to the finance community by demonstrating the applicability of the Vanna-Volga method through theory development, practical implementation and empirical assessment. Although the underlying theory is not as rigorous as other advanced option valuation frameworks, the Vanna-Volga method has been equipped with sufficient building blocks to allow the theory to be extended to VaR amount calculation and dynamic portfolio replication from solely currency option valuation. The practical implementation aims at demonstrating that the Vanna-Volga method is a cost-effective alternative because of the availability of closed-form solutions and the leveraging of the financial information services currently available for the Black-Scholes model, in contrast to other advanced models that lack closed-form solutions and for which calibration of model parameters has to be performed by the financial institutions themselves. The empirical assessment objectively measures how much improvement is introduced by this low-cost alternative to the baseline case. Through complete theory development, cost-effective implementation and high accuracy, the Vanna-Volga method is ascertained to be a highly practical industry solution.

On the other hand, while previous research on the Vanna-Volga method has largely focused on currency option valuation, this study essentially extends the method's application to VaR amount calculation and dynamic portfolio replication in order to arrive at a total solution for managing currency options under a unified theoretical framework.

Finally, this study also justifies the Vanna-Volga method through examining the improvements it offers over classical market practices. By comparing the potential improvements and the cost, the benefits of the Vanna-Volga method are readily observed.

Note

1 Professor Fisher Black passed away in 1995.

2 Development of theories on currency option management

This chapter summarizes the historical development of the theories on the management of currency options, covering the definition of currency options, the Black-Scholes option valuation model, the volatility smile, value-at-risk (VaR) and dynamic portfolio replication.

2.1 Vanilla European currency options

A vanilla European currency call option (Call Option) is a financial contract between an acquirer and a writer. The acquirer of a Call Option has the right but not the obligation to buy an agreed quantity of an underlying currency from the writer with a strike rate K at maturity T. The writer, in turn, is obligated to sell the agreed quantity of the underlying currency to the acquirer at strike rate K upon maturity T. The acquirer is benefited if the market rate of the underlying currency moves above the strike rate at maturity so that he can buy the underlying currency at a rate K lower than the market rate at maturity $S(T)$. Mathematically, the payoff of a long position in a Call Option with strike rate K at maturity T is expressed as:

$$Payoff\left[Call\right] = Max\left[S(T) - K, 0\right] \tag{2.1}$$

A vanilla European currency put option (Put Option) is another type of financial contract between an acquirer and a writer. The acquirer of a Put Option has the right but not the obligation to sell an agreed quantity of an underlying currency to the writer with a strike rate K at maturity T. The writer, in turn, is obligated to buy the agreed quantity of the underlying currency from the acquirer at strike rate K upon maturity T. The acquirer is benefited if the market rate of the underlying currency is below the strike rate so that he can sell the underlying currency at a rate K higher than the market rate at maturity $S(T)$. Mathematically, the payoff of a long position in a Put Option with strike rate K at maturity T is expressed as:

$$Payoff\left[Put\right] = Max\left[K - S(T), 0\right] \tag{2.2}$$

In order to acquire a currency option that will provide a monetary benefit, the currency option acquirer must pay a premium to the currency option writer, who will be obligated to deliver the monetary benefit at maturity. To determine the fair amount of the premium, which is essentially the value of a currency option, a methodology is required. This has triggered a large amount of research on currency option valuation (Black and Scholes, 1973; Merton, 1973).

Moreover, since currency options are OTC derivatives of which the specification is highly customized between an acquirer and a writer, it is rare that the market price of a currency option with identical specification can be observed directly from financial information providers. Therefore, for practical reasons, currency options are valuated by option valuating models with relevant and observable independent variables as input parameters rather than by marking-to-market.

2.2 Black-Scholes model

The Black-Scholes model is by far the most popular valuation methodology being utilized by practitioners in currency option trading. The model was first proposed by Black and Scholes (1973) and further extended by Merton (1973).

2.2.1 Currency option valuation

Under the Black-Scholes model, the evolution of the value of an underlying currency is assumed to follow a geometric Brownian motion in a risk-neutral world with constant volatility σ, constant domestic risk-free rate r_u and constant foreign risk-free rate r_{f}, that is,

$$dS(t) = S(t)(r_d - r_f)dt + S(t)\sigma dW(t) \tag{2.3}$$

where *W(t)* is a Wiener process.

With these assumptions in place, the Call Option value *c(t)* and Put Option value *p(t)* can be calculated with the following two formulas:

$$c(t) = S(t)\exp\left[-r_f(T-t)\right]\Phi\left[d_1(t)\right]$$
$$- K\exp\left[-r_d(T-t)\right]\Phi\left[d_2(t)\right] \tag{2.4}$$

$$p(t) = K\exp\left[-r_d(T-t)\right]\Phi\left[-d_2(t)\right]$$
$$- S(t)\exp\left[-r_f(T-t)\right]\Phi\left[-d_1(t)\right] \tag{2.5}$$

where

$$d_1(t) = \frac{\ln\left[\dfrac{S(t)}{K}\right] + \left(r_d - r_f + \dfrac{\sigma^2}{2}\right)(T - t)}{\sigma\sqrt{T - t}}$$

$$d_2(t) = d_1(t) - \sigma\sqrt{T - t}$$

$$\Phi(x) = \int_{-\infty}^{x} \frac{1}{\sqrt{2\pi}} \exp\left(-\frac{s^2}{2}\right) ds \tag{2.6}$$

These famous Black-Scholes formulas and the underlying framework laid the foundation for modern option valuating theory and became the standard language in the market of currency option trading.

2.2.2 Greeks

Greeks are the sensitivity measures of the change in a currency option's value relative to the change in one or more independent variables. They are frequently utilized to assess the impact on currency option value of small fluctuations in an independent variable, for example the market rate of the underlying currency and/or volatility. In addition, Greeks are also adopted in Taylor series to approximate the change in currency option price resulting from a small change in the independent variables.

For a currency option with a maturity of less than one year, the impact on currency option value arising from changes in domestic and/or foreign interest rates is relatively immaterial (Castagna, 2010), leaving only the market price of the underlying currency and volatility as the two critical independent variables. Based on the Black-Scholes formulas, the major Greeks are derived and listed in Table 2.1, with *V(t)* being the currency option value.

2.2.3 Taylor expansion

With the Greeks in place, subject to the assumption that the higher order terms will converge to zero, the theory of Taylor expansion suggests that

- The small change in currency option value driven by a small change in the underlying currency rate could be approximated by a Taylor series:

$$V\left[S(t) + dS(t)\right] = V\left[S(t)\right] + \frac{\partial V\left[S(t)\right]}{\partial S(t)} dS(t)$$

$$+ \frac{1}{2} \frac{\partial V\left[S(t)\right]}{\partial S(t)^2} \left[dS(t)\right]^2 + \cdots$$

$$= V\left[S(t)\right] + Delta \cdot dS(t) + \frac{Gamma}{2}\left[dS(t)\right]^2 + \cdots \tag{2.7}$$

Table 2.1 Major Greeks for currency options

	Greek	Definition	Formula
11	Delta	$\dfrac{\partial V(t)}{\partial S(t)}$	$\exp\left[-r_f(T-t)\right]\Phi\left[d_1(t)\right]$ (call)
			$\exp\left[-r_f(T-t)\right]\Phi\left[d_1(t)\right]$ $-\exp\left[r_f(T-t)\right]$ (put)
22	Gamma	$\dfrac{\partial^2 V(t)}{\partial S(t)^2}$	$\dfrac{\exp\left[-r_f(T-t)\right]\phi\left[d_1(t)\right]}{S(t)\sigma\sqrt{T-t}}$ $=\dfrac{Vega}{\left[S(t)\right]^2\sigma(T-t)}$
33	Speed	$\dfrac{\partial^3 V(t)}{\partial S(t)^3}$	$-\dfrac{\exp\left[-r_f(T-t)\right]\phi\left[d_1(t)\right]}{\left[S(t)\right]^2\sigma\sqrt{T-t}}$ $\left[\dfrac{d_1(t)}{\sigma\sqrt{T-t}}+1\right]$ $=-\dfrac{Gamma}{S(t)}\left[\dfrac{d_1(t)}{\sigma\sqrt{T-t}}+1\right]$
44	Vega	$\dfrac{\partial V(t)}{\partial \sigma}$	$S(t)\exp\left[-r_f(T-t)\right]\phi\left[d_1(t)\right]\sqrt{T-t}$ $=K\exp\left[-r_d(T-t)\right]\phi\left[d_2(t)\right]\sqrt{T-t}$
55	Volga	$\dfrac{\partial^2 V(t)}{\partial \sigma^2}$	$\dfrac{S(t)\exp\left[-r_f(T-t)\right]\phi\left[d_1(t)\right]\cdot d_1(t)d_2(t)\sqrt{T-t}}{\sigma}$ $=\dfrac{Vega\cdot d_1(t)d_2(t)}{\sigma}$
66	Ultima	$\dfrac{\partial^3 V(t)}{\partial \sigma^3}$	$-\dfrac{Vega\cdot\begin{Bmatrix}d_1(t)d_2(t)\left[1-d_1(t)d_2(t)\right]\\+\left[d_1(t)\right]^2+\left[d_2(t)\right]^2\end{Bmatrix}}{\sigma^2}$
77	Vanna	$\dfrac{\partial V^2(t)}{\partial S(t)\partial \sigma}$	$-\exp\left[-r_f(T-t)\right]\phi\left[d_1(t)\right]d_2(t)$ $=-\dfrac{Vega\cdot d_2(t)}{S(t)\sigma\sqrt{T-t}}$

- A small change in currency option value driven by the small change in volatility could be approximated by a similar Taylor series:

$$V(\sigma + d\sigma) = V(\sigma) + \frac{\partial V(\sigma)}{\partial \sigma} d\sigma + \frac{1}{2} \frac{\partial V(\sigma)}{\partial \sigma^2} d\sigma^2 + \cdots$$

$$= V(\sigma) + Vega \cdot d\sigma + \frac{Volga}{2} \cdot d\sigma^2 + \cdots \tag{2.8}$$

2.3 Implied volatility

Volatility is essentially a quantity not directly observable from the financial market. In contrast, the market prices of liquidly traded currency options are readily available from actual transactions. Therefore, in practice, Black-Scholes formulas are utilized to back out the volatility of most liquidly traded currency options. This volatility backed out from the Black-Sholes formulas is referred to as implied volatility, which is then adopted in Black-Scholes formulas again to calculate the values of other, less liquidly traded but similar currency options. This process becomes a standard procedure for practitioners to valuate illiquid financial instruments with their liquidly traded family members.

In general, the most liquidly traded currency options are those with strike rates close to the market rate of the underlying currency. These currency options are referred to as at-the-money (ATM) currency options.

To facilitate the ease of subsequent mathematical formulation, an ATM currency option is technically defined as follows: if a Call Option and a Put Option, both with the same underlying currency, same maturity T and same strike rate K, have the same magnitude of Delta in opposite signs, then these two currency options are ATM options at strike rate K.

Given the volatility of an ATM currency option, the strike rate is calculated as:

$$K_{ATM} = S(t) \exp \left[\left(r_d - r_f \right)(T - t) + \frac{\sigma_{ATM}^2 (T - t)}{2} \right] \tag{2.9}$$

2.3.1 Volatility smile

A number of empirical studies (Heston, 1993; Corrado and Su, 1996) have demonstrated that if prices of Call Options and Put Options with the same underlying currency and maturity but with different strike rates are collected from traded transactions and substituted into the Black-Scholes formulas to back out the corresponding volatilities, the volatilities essentially exhibit as a convex function of strike rate in a smile shape, hence the name 'volatility smile'. The observation of volatility smiles is inconsistent with the Black-Scholes model's assumption of single constant volatility.

2.3.2 Volatility surface

For the same underlying currency, a collection of volatility smiles with different maturities forms a volatility surface. Theoretically, there are an infinite number of points on the volatility surface, corresponding to different combinations of maturities and strike rates. In practice, financial information providers describe this volatility surface in a two-dimensional grid convention, that is an implied volatility is exhibited at each combination of standard maturity and standard moneyness.

(a) Standard maturity: Standard maturities include one day, one week, two weeks, one month, two months, three months, six months, nine months, one year, two years, five years and ten years.

(b) Standard moneyness: Moneyness is a measure of how far the strike rate is from the market rate of the underlying currency. In the currency option market, moneyness is specified by Delta of a currency option. A Call Option with a low positive Delta or a Put Option with a low negative Delta indicates that the strike rate is far from market rate of the underlying currency. In contrast, a Call Option with a moderate positive Delta or a Put Option with a moderate negative Delta indicates that the strike rate is close to the market rate of the underlying currency. Standard moneynesses include ATM, 10-Delta, 15-Delta, 25-Delta and 35-Delta. A right d-Delta Call means a Call Option with Delta d% and a left d-Delta Put means a Put Option with Delta-d%. A left d-Delta Call means a Call Option with Delta $\exp\left[-r_f\left(T-t\right)\right]-d\%$ and a right d-Delta Put means a Put Option with Delta $d\%-\exp\left[-r_f\left(T-t\right)\right]$.

(c) For a Call Option, the strike rate and Delta are related by the following formula:

$$Delta_c = \exp\left[-r_f\left(T-t\right)\right]\Phi\left[d_1\left(t\right)\right]$$

$$K = S\exp\left\langle \begin{matrix} \left(r_d-r_f\right)\left(T-t\right)+\dfrac{\sigma^2\left(T-t\right)}{2} \\ -\Phi^{-1}\left\{Delta_c\cdot\exp\left[r_f\left(T-t\right)\right]\right\}\cdot\sigma\sqrt{T} \end{matrix} \right\rangle \qquad (2.10)$$

For a Put Option, its Delta is first converted to the Delta of a corresponding Call Option through this relationship:

$$Call\ Delta = \exp\left[-r_f\left(T-t\right)\right]+Put\ Delta \qquad (2.11)$$

and Equation 2.10 is then applied to calculate the strike rate.

For currency options with standard maturity and standard moneyness, the volatilities are readily available from major financial information services providers.

This makes the volatility surface an important input in the management of currency options.

2.4 Trader's rule of thumb

The existence of volatility smile and volatility surface indicates the imperfection of the Black-Scholes model. Practitioners seek to improve the Black-Scholes model because of its simplicity and tractability and the large number of services already developed with respect to the Black-Scholes model. This results in the trader's rule of thumb (TROT), which is essentially an *ad hoc* correction to the Black-Scholes model in accordance with practitioners' general practice in characterizing a volatility smile with readily available market quotes from financial information providers.

2.4.1 25-Delta risk reversal and 25-Delta butterfly

The TROT is developed with respect to two liquidly traded currency option structures in the market: 25-Delta risk reversal and 25-Delta butterfly.

(a) A 25-Delta risk reversal is a portfolio comprising:

- A long position in a right 25-Delta Call Option; and
- A short potion in a left 25-Delta Put Option,

both with the same underlying currency and same maturity. The formula for this is:

$$RR(t) = c_{+25}(t) - p_{-25}(t) \tag{2.12}$$

A 25-Delta risk reversal has Delta 50 percent and significant Vanna but immaterial Volga.

(b) A 25-Delta butterfly is a portfolio comprising:

- Half long position in a right 25-Delta Call Option;
- Half long position in a left 25-Delta Put Option;
- Half short position in an ATM Call Option; and
- Half short position in an ATM Put Option,

all with the same underlying currency and same maturity, that is:

$$BF(t) = \frac{c_{+25}(t) + p_{-25}(t) - c_{ATM}(t) - p_{ATM}(t)}{2} \tag{2.13}$$

A 25-Delta butterfly has zero Delta, significant Volga and immaterial Vanna.

2.4.2 Currency option valuation

With these elementary option structures in place, the TROT suggests the value of a currency option calculated as shown in Formula 2.14 (Wystup, 2008):

$$V^{TROT}(t) = V^{BS}(t) + w_{RR}(t)\left[RR^{Market}(t) - RR^{BS}(t)\right]$$
$$+ w_{BF}(t)\left[BF^{Market}(t) - BF^{BS}(t)\right]$$

$$w_{RR}(t) = \frac{\dfrac{\partial^2 V^{BS}(t)}{\partial S(t)\partial\sigma_{ATM}}}{\dfrac{\partial^2 RR^{BS}(t)}{\partial S(t)\partial\sigma_{ATM}}} = \frac{\dfrac{\partial^2 V^{BS}(t)}{\partial S(t)\partial\sigma_{ATM}}}{\dfrac{\partial^2 c_{+25}^{BS}(t)}{\partial S(t)\partial\sigma_{ATM}} - \dfrac{\partial^2 p_{-25}^{BS}}{\partial S(t)\partial\sigma_{ATM}}}$$

$$w_{BF}(t) = \frac{\dfrac{\partial^2 V^{BS}(t)}{\partial\sigma_{ATM}^2}}{\dfrac{\partial^2 BF^{BS}(t)}{\partial\sigma_{ATM}^2}} = \frac{\dfrac{\partial^2 V^{BS}(t)}{\partial\sigma_{ATM}^2}}{\dfrac{\partial^2 c_{+25}^{BS}(t)}{\partial\sigma_{ATM}^2} + \dfrac{\partial^2 p_{-25}^{BS}(t)}{\partial\sigma_{ATM}^2} - \dfrac{\partial^2 c_{ATM}^{BS}(t)}{\partial\sigma_{ATM}^2} - \dfrac{\partial^2 p_{ATM}^{BS}(t)}{\partial\sigma_{ATM}^2}}$$

$$RR^{Market}(t) = c_{+25}^{Market}(t) - p_{-25}^{Market}(t)$$
$$RR^{BS}(t) = c_{+25}^{BS}(t) - p_{-25}^{BS}(t)$$

$$BF^{Market}(t) = \frac{c_{+25}^{Market}(t) + p_{-25}^{Market}(t) - c_{ATM}^{Market}(t) - p_{ATM}^{Market}(t)}{2}$$
$$BF^{BS}(t) = \frac{c_{+25}^{BS}(t) + p_{-25}^{BS}(t) - c_{ATM}^{BS}(t) - p_{ATM}^{BS}(t)}{2} \tag{2.14}$$

where the superscript 'Market' represents a price observed from the financial market and the superscript 'BS' represents a value calculated by the Black-Scholes formulas with ATM volatility. The TROT option valuation formula is derived from the experience of currency option traders, without a formal standing in option valuation theory.

Due to this *ad hoc* construction, the TROT option valuation formula does not produce values consistent with the prices of ATM Call Option, ATM Put Option, 25-Delta Call Option and 25-Delta Put Option derived directly from the volatilities at standard moneyness (Bossens, Rayée, Skantzos and Deelstra, 2010). This internal inconsistency limits the theoretical development of the TROT. Having said that, the TROT marked a new direction for improving the accuracy of currency option valuation by considering the extra readily available information from liquidly traded current options in addition to the ATM currency options. The idea behind it is quite intuitive: the liquidly traded currency options with standard maturities and standard moneyness provide additional information about the dynamics of the volatility surface. As such, they are essentially fundamental financial instruments that can be utilized to improve the accuracy of the Black-Scholes model.

2.5 Malz formula

In response to demand from the currency option market, where there is a need to derive a volatility smile quickly from very few readily available market quotes, Malz (1997) proposed a simple second-order polynomial to fit a volatility smile by the Delta of a Call Option:

$$\sigma = \sigma_{ATM} - 2\sigma_{RR}\left(Delta - \frac{1}{2}\right) + 16\sigma_{BF}\left(Delta - \frac{1}{2}\right)^2 \tag{2.15}$$

where

$$\sigma_{RR} = \sigma_{+25} - \sigma_{-25}$$
$$\sigma_{BF} = \frac{\sigma_{+25} + \sigma_{-25}}{2} - \sigma_{ATM}$$

Reiswich and Wystup (2009) provided a correction to Equation 2.15:

$$\sigma = \sigma_{ATM} - 2\sigma_{RR}\left\{Delta\cdot\exp\left[r_f\left(T - t\right)\right] - \frac{1}{2}\right\}$$
$$+ 16\sigma_{BF}\left\{Delta\cdot\exp\left[r_f\left(T - t\right)\right] - \frac{1}{2}\right\}^2 \tag{2.16}$$

A major paradox of the Malz formula is that while the volatility of an option with a given Delta can be calculated with the formula, the Delta of an option can be obtained only when the volatility is available. Thus the practical application of the Malz formula is limited.

2.6 Value-at-risk

VaR is the most popular quantitative measure of market risk in financial institutions. It is widely used in market risk management and in reporting of capital charges for market risk under the Basel II framework. Risk managers use VaR to set market risk limits, and bank supervisors use VaR to ensure that banks hold sufficient regulatory capital against their exposures to market risk.

For a financial instrument, VaR describes the loss that will not be exceeded at a high confidence level over a short trading period. In general, financial instruments with higher market risk exhibit a higher value of VaR. Thus VaR is also applicable to measuring market risk of currency options.

2.6.1 VaR amount at the 99th percentile confidence level over a one-day horizon

A VaR amount at the 99th percentile confidence level over a one-day horizon (one-day VaR amount) is defined as the potential loss that would not be exceeded with 99 percent probability if a currency option were held static over one trading day.

Under the Black-Scholes model, the dominating market risk factor of a currency option is the market rate of the underlying currency. For a single currency, based on the assumption that the currency rate follows a geometric Brownian motion, the one-day VaR amount is estimated to be 2.325 times the market rate of the currency, according to J.P. Morgan (1994).

For a currency option, following Equation 2.7, the change in the option value can be approximated by the first-order differential:

$$dV\left[S(t)\right] \approx Delta \cdot dS(t) = Delta \cdot S(t) \cdot \frac{dS(t)}{S(t)} \tag{2.17}$$

Therefore, the one-day VaR amount can be calculated with this linear approximation:

$$\text{One-day VaR amount} \approx 2.3263 \cdot Delta \cdot S(t) \tag{2.18}$$

This formulation of the one-day VaR amount calculation for currency option is referred to as Delta-normal VaR, which characterizes the one-day VaR amount of a currency option as a simple linear function of the market value of the currency rate. This linear approximation is convenient when calculating the one-day VaR amount of a portfolio of currency options.

2.6.2 Forecasting of standard deviation

The standard deviation of daily change in a risk factor measures the dispersion of a risk factor around its expected value. A higher standard deviation indicates a larger potential fluctuation in a risk factor. As such, forecasting of forward looking standard deviations pays a critical role in calculating the one-day VaR amounts.

Under the assumption that a risk factor A is a random variable, the standard deviation of the risk factor SD is defined as:

$$SD = \sqrt{E\left[\left(A - E[A]\right)^2\right]} = E\left[A^2\right] - \left(E[A]\right)^2 \tag{2.19}$$

There are two common approaches to forecasting standard deviations, namely the simple moving average (SMA) model and the exponentially weighted moving average (EWMA) model (Hull, 2008).

The SMA model assumes that the squared standard deviation of a risk factor in the next time period $N + 1$ is forecast by the arithmetic average of the squared standard deviation of the risk factor X for previous N time periods, that is:

$$SD_{N+1}^2 = \frac{\sum_{k=1}^{N} x_k^2}{N} \tag{2.20}$$

It is very easy to estimate a standard deviation under the SMA model. Neverthe-less, the standard deviation forecast by the SMA model suffers from the choice of number of days N. A larger N results in a statistically sufficient and stable standard deviation forecast, with a certain amount of outdated historical values incorporated. On the other hand, a smaller N ensures that most of the values utilized for standard deviation forecasting are up to date, but at the expenses of lower statistical suffi-ciency and stability. Moreover, the ghost effect due to the injection and retirement of any large value in the time window N days creates an abrupt change in the stand-ard deviation forecast on the injection day and retirement day (Alexander, 2009).

J.P. Morgan (1994) proposed the EWMA model where the current squared standard deviation forecast is updated by the most recent value of the risk factor in order to arrive at a new standard deviation forecast, that is:

$$SD_{N+1}^2 = \lambda \cdot SD_N^2 + \left(1 - \lambda\right) x_N^2 \tag{2.21}$$

where λ is a decay factor between 0 and 1.

The EWMA model provides the freedom to recognize the relevance of the most recent value of the risk factor to the latest standard deviation forecast by assigning a decay factor in the equation. J.P. Morgan set the decay factor λ to 0.94 in its famous RiskMetrics implementation for forecasting standard devia-tions. Although the choice of λ is a bit *ad hoc*, the EWMA model has been well received by the banking industry, since the ghost effect of the SMA model has been effectively addressed (Berkowitz and O'Brien, 2002).

2.6.3 Back testing

Back testing is conducted by comparing a one-day VaR amount calculated on the previous trading day with the actual loss observed on the current trading day, assuming that the financial instrument is held static between two consecutive trading days (BCBS, 2009). If the actual loss on the current trading day exceeds the one-day VaR amount calculated at the end of previous trading day, a violation is registered.

In a statistical sense, a VaR model is considered to be accurate if over a sufficiently long period of trading days the percentage of trading days on which violations are registered approaches 1 percent. Nevertheless, a validation based on this definition is less practical since over a long period a market-insensitive VaR model that overestimates one-day VaR amounts during tranquil periods and underestimates one-day VaR amounts during volatile periods may show the overestimations offsetting the underestimations, resulting in a satisfactory back testing performance. Yet this market-insensitive VaR model is not useful for market risk management (Hair, Black, Babin, Andeson and Tatham, 2006). Therefore, for practical reasons, BCBS (2009) adopts back testing over a period comprising the most recent 250 consecutive trading days.

2.7 Dynamic portfolio replication

In additional to currency option valuation, the Black-Scholes model also suggests a methodology for replicating a currency option with its underlying currency and cash (Hull, 2008).

Under the assumption that the risk-free rates r_d and r_f are constant, for a currency option X, the Black-Scholes model suggests the following replication strategy:

- At time t, a replicating portfolio $R(t)$ of currency option X is formed with (i) a $Delta(t)$ unit of underlying currency and (ii) a domestic cash amount $z(t)$ being put in a money market account, that is;

$$V(t) = R(t) = Delta(t)S(t) + z(t) \qquad (2.22)$$

- At time $t + dt$, the replicating portfolio evolves to $R(t + dt)$ and comprises (i) $Delta(t)$ units of underlying currency, (ii) the interest amount $Delta(t)S(t)r_f dt$ generated by the underlying currency, and (iii) domestic cash amount $(1 + r_f dt)z(t)$ in a money market account, that is:

$$R(t + dt) = Delta(t)S(t + dt) + Delta(t)S(t)r_f dt$$
$$+ (1 + r_d dt)z(t) \qquad (2.23)$$

This replicating portfolio is then rebalanced with $Delta(t + dt)$ units of underlying currency. The cash surplus or deficit as a result of rebalancing is deposited to or withdrawn from the money market account to arrive at a new domestic cash amount $z(t + dt)$. This forms a self-finance trading strategy, and the value of the replicating portfolio must be the same as the value of the currency option $V(t + dt)$, that is:

$$V(t + dt) = R(t + dt) = Delta(t + dt)S(t + dt) + z(t + dt) \qquad (2.24)$$

- The rebalancing process is repeated continuously until maturity T. Then the terminal payoff of currency option X should be equal to the sum of (i) the value of the underlying currency and (ii) the amount of domestic cash in the money market account, that is:

$$Payoff[X] = R(T) = Delta(T)S(T) + z(T)$$
$$= Delta(T)Payoff[X_k] + z(T) \qquad (2.25)$$

In practice, dynamic portfolio replication can be performed only on a discrete time basis, for example once a day. Moreover, the slight shift of risk-free rates may also affect the performance of replication, although the difference is immaterial.

2.7.1 Temporal interpolation

Theoretically, every maturity is equipped with its own volatility smile for a particular currency. Nevertheless, financial information providers publish only the volatilities at certain moneynesses and standard maturities of one day, one week, two week, one month, two months, three months, six months, nine months, one year, two years, five years and ten years. This imposes a challenge to the valuation of currency options at nonstandard maturities.

In order to arrive at the volatilities between any two standard maturities, Clark (2011) proposed a simple procedure for interpolating the entire volatility surface, referred to as the total variance interpolation method, which suggests that the ATM and wing volatilities at a nonstandard maturity can be interpolated with this formula:

$$\sigma(T) = \sqrt{\frac{T - T_k}{T_{k+1} - T_k} \cdot \frac{T_{k+1}}{T} \cdot \left[\sigma(T_{k+1})\right]^2 + \frac{T_{k+1} - T}{T_{k+1} - T_k} \cdot \frac{T_k}{T} \cdot \left[\sigma(T_k)\right]^2} \qquad (2.26)$$

where T is any nonstandard maturity between standard maturities T_k and T_{k+1}.

A fine-tuning is made by applying relative weights to trading days and nontrading days:

- Count the number of days N_1 between T_k and T;
- Count the number of days N_2 between T_k and T_{k+1};
- Assign a weight 1 to trading days;
- Assign a weight 0.5 to a nontrading days;
- Define $\tau_1 = \sum_{k=1}^{N_1} w_k$, $\tau_2 = \sum_{k=1}^{N_2} w_k$;

- Then Equation 2.26 is refined to:

$$\sigma(T) = \sqrt{\frac{\tau_1}{\tau_2} \cdot \frac{T_{k+1}}{T} \cdot \left[\sigma(T_{k+1})\right]^2 + \frac{\tau_2 - \tau_1}{\tau_2} \cdot \frac{T_k}{T} \cdot \left[\sigma(T_k)\right]^2}$$

(2.27)

2.8 Benchmarking

In the subsequent analysis, the Black-Scholes model and its relevant properties will be adopted as the benchmarks for demonstrating the improvements represented by the Vanna-Volga method over the Black-Scholes model. The choice of using Black-Scholes model is obvious because:

- Both the Vanna-Volga method and the Black-Scholes model belong to the group practitioners' model, which (i) can be expressed in closed-form solutions to facilitate fast computation; (ii) uses readily available data from financial information providers to calculate the currency option value; (ii) does not need calibration on model specific parameters. Other stochastic option valuation models generally lack such nice properties.
- In term of the theory, the Vanna-Volga method is indeed a correction to the Black-Scholes model, which assumes a single constant volatility.

3 Volatility recovery

Volatility recovery is the process of deriving the volatility of a less liquidly traded currency option with a few market observable parameters in accordance with some methodologies, given the maturity and moneyness of that particular currency option. This recovered volatility can then be utilized to derive the value of other currency options and exotic currency options with similar maturity and moneyness. As such, volatility recovery plays a critical role in the study of currency option valuation.

While many volatility recovery approaches have been proposed during the past two decades, all volatility recovery approaches except the Malz formula require some form of model calibration with numerical methods to recover the model parameters before the volatility is recovered. This computationally intensive limitation makes them less practical in real-life implementation.

Castagna and Mercurio (2007) proposed a new methodology, namely the Vanna-Volga method, which seeks to recover volatilities with readily available currency rates, interest rates and standard volatilities, thus eliminating the involvement of model calibration.

3.1 Theoretical framework

This section sets out the theoretical framework of the Vanna-Volga method, leveraging the foundations of literatures reviewed previously in Chapter 2. The Vanna-Volga option valuating framework and the related technical details are derived, riding on the argument of dynamic portfolio replication similar to the Delta hedging adopted in the Black-Scholes model.

3.1.1 Fundamental problem

The fundamental problem of currency option valuation with the Vanna-Volga method is formalized as follows: at time t, for the same underlying currency with market rate $S(t)$ and the same time to maturity T, there are three liquidly traded vanilla European currency options X_1, X_2 and X_3 with strike rates $K_1 < K_2 < K_3$ respectively. These currency options share the same constant Black-Scholes volatility σ_{BS} in order to arrive at their Black-Scholes values, calculated in accordance with the Black-Scholes formulas. The market prices of the currency options X_1, X_2 and X_3 are observed to be $V_1(t)$, $V_2(t)$ and $V_3(t)$, which are then input into the

Black-Scholes formulas to back out three different implied volatilities σ_1, σ_2 and σ_3, respectively. The constant domestic risk-free rate is r_d and the constant foreign risk-free rate is r_f. What is the value $V(t)$ of a new vanilla European currency option X with the same underlying currency at market rate $S(t)$, the same time to maturity T and an arbitrary strike rate K?

3.1.1.1 Replicating portfolio

Since the implied volatilities σ_1, σ_2 and σ_3 are different from the Black-Scholes volatility σ_{BS}, the assumption of single constant volatility in the Black-Scholes model is violated. Castagna and Mercurio (2007) proposed a correction to the Black-Scholes model by forming a replicating portfolio to neutralize four Greeks – Delta, Vega, Vanna and Volga of the new currency option X with the underlying currency and three liquidly traded currency options.

This currency option X is hedged with an offsetting position of a replicating portfolio comprising the underlying currency and three liquidly traded options X_1, X_2 and X_3 where $w_0(t)$, $w_1(t)$, $w_2(t)$ and $w_3(t)$ are the hedging ratios to form a Delta, Vega, Vanna and Volga neutral portfolio Π (t) within an infinitesimal short period of time, that is:

Currency option – replicating portfolio = Risk-free security

$$V(t) - \left[w_0(t)S(t) + \sum_{k=1}^{3} w_k(t)V_k(t) \right] = \Pi(t)$$

$$\sum_{k=1}^{3} w_k(t)V_k(t) = V(t) - w_0(t)S(t) - \Pi(t)$$

(3.1)

Consider the moment at $T - dt$, an infinitesimal short time dt before maturity T.

- If the replicating portfolio $\Pi(T - dt)$ is constructed by the currency options in market prices, then:

$$\Pi^{Market}(T - dt) = V^{Market}(T - dt) - w_0(T - dt) \cdot S(T - dt)$$
$$- \sum_{k=1}^{3} w_k(T - dt)V_k^{Market}(T - dt)$$

(3.2)

- If the replicating portfolio $\Pi(T - dt)$ is constructed by the currency options in Black-Scholes values, then:

$$\Pi^{BS}(T - dt) = V^{BS}(T - dt) - w_0(T - dt) \cdot S(T - dt)$$
$$- \sum_{k=1}^{3} w_k(T - dt)V_k^{BS}(T - dt)$$

(3.3)

At maturity T, the payoff of the replicating portfolio $\Pi(T)$, whether it is constructed by the currency options in market prices or according to Black-Scholes values, becomes:

$$\Pi^{Market}(T) = \Pi^{BS}(T)$$

$$= V(T) - w_0(T - dt)S(T) - \sum_{k=1}^{3} w_k(T - dt)V_k(T)$$

$$= Payoff[X] - w_0(T - dt)S(T)$$

$$- \sum_{k=1}^{3} w_k(T - dt)Payoff[X_k] \tag{3.4}$$

By the no-arbitrage argument, if the two replicating portfolios have the same payoff at maturity T, then these two replicating portfolios must have the same value at time $T - dt$. Thus:

$$\Pi^{Market}(T - dt) = \Pi^{BS}(T - dt) \tag{3.5}$$

Assume the hedging ratios $w_0(t)$, $w_1(t)$, $w_2(t)$ and $w_3(t)$ are recalibrated continuously and evolve smoothly, that is:

$$\begin{bmatrix} w_0(t - dt) \\ w_1(t - dt) \\ w_2(t - dt) \\ w_3(t - dt) \end{bmatrix} \approx \begin{bmatrix} w_0(t) \\ w_1(t) \\ w_2(t) \\ w_3(t) \end{bmatrix} \tag{3.6}$$

by repeating this backward induction and no-arbitrage argument at time $T - 2dt$, $T - 3dt$, $T - 4dt$, . . . at any time t before maturity T,

$$\Pi^{Market}(t) = \Pi^{BS}(t) = \Pi(t) \tag{3.7}$$

that is, equality (3.1) is held for both the market prices and Black-Scholes values of the currency options, then:

$$\sum_{k=1}^{3} w_k(t)V_k^{Market}(t) = V^{Market}(t) - w_0(t)S(t) - \Pi^{Market}(t) \tag{3.8}$$

$$\sum_{k=1}^{3} w_k(t) V_k^{BS}(t) = V^{BS}(t) - w_0(t) S(t) - \Pi^{BS}(t)$$

(3.9)

The difference between equations (3.8) and (3.9) becomes:

$$V^{Market}(t) - V^{BS}(t) = \sum_{k=1}^{3} w_k(t) \left[V_k^{Market}(t) - V_k^{BS}(t) \right]$$

$$V^{Market}(t) = V^{BS}(t) + \sum_{k=1}^{3} w_k(t) \left[V_k^{Market}(t) - V_k^{BS}(t) \right]$$

(3.10)

The Vanna-Volga currency option valuation formula simply states that in order to arrive at the market price $V^{Market}(t)$ of currency option X, the Black-Scholes value $V^{BS}(t)$ should be corrected, taking into account (i) the difference between the market prices and the Black-Scholes values of the three liquidly traded currency options, and (ii) the hedging ratios.

3.1.1.2 Hedging ratios

Under the assumption that there exists a single Black-Scholes volatility for these four options X_1, X_2, X_3 and X, taking the:

- First derivative of equation (3.10) with respect to the Black-Scholes volatility σ_{BS};
- Second derivative of equation (3.10) with respect to the market rate of underlying currency $S(t)$ and Black-Scholes volatility σ_{BS}; and
- Second derivative of equation (3.10) with respect to the Black-Scholes volatility σ_{BS}, the following system of linear equations, in matrix form, is derived:

$$
\begin{bmatrix}
\dfrac{\partial V_1^{BS}(t)}{\partial \sigma_{BS}} & \dfrac{\partial V_2^{BS}(t)}{\partial \sigma_{BS}} & \dfrac{\partial V_3^{BS}(t)}{\partial \sigma_{BS}} \\[2ex]
\dfrac{\partial^2 V_1^{BS}(t)}{\partial S(t)\partial \sigma_{BS}} & \dfrac{\partial^2 V_2^{BS}(t)}{\partial S(t)\partial \sigma_{BS}} & \dfrac{\partial^2 V_2^{BS}(t)}{\partial S(t)\partial \sigma_{BS}} \\[2ex]
\dfrac{\partial^2 V_1^{BS}(t)}{\partial \sigma_{BS}^2} & \dfrac{\partial^2 V_2^{BS}(t)}{\partial \sigma_{BS}^2} & \dfrac{\partial^2 V_2^{BS}(t)}{\partial \sigma_{BS}^2}
\end{bmatrix}
\begin{bmatrix}
w_1(t) \\[1ex] w_2(t) \\[1ex] w_3(t)
\end{bmatrix}
=
\begin{bmatrix}
\dfrac{\partial V^{BS}(t)}{\partial \sigma_{BS}} \\[2ex]
\dfrac{\partial^2 V^{BS}(t)}{\partial S(t)\partial \sigma_{BS}} \\[2ex]
\dfrac{\partial^2 V^{BS}(t)}{\partial \sigma_{BS}^2}
\end{bmatrix}
$$

(3.11)

Castagna and Mercurio (2007) derived an elegant closed-form solution to the system of linear equations (3.11):

$$
\begin{bmatrix} w_1(t) \\ w_2(t) \\ w_3(t) \end{bmatrix} =
\begin{bmatrix}
\dfrac{\partial V^{BS}(t)}{\partial \sigma_{BS}} \cdot \ln \dfrac{K_2}{K} \cdot \ln \dfrac{K_3}{K} \\[2ex]
\dfrac{\partial V_1^{BS}(t)}{\partial \sigma_{BS}} \cdot \ln \dfrac{K_2}{K_1} \cdot \ln \dfrac{K_3}{K_1} \\[2ex]
\dfrac{\partial V^{BS}(t)}{\partial \sigma_{BS}} \cdot \ln \dfrac{K}{K_1} \cdot \ln \dfrac{K_3}{K} \\[2ex]
\dfrac{\partial V_2^{BS}(t)}{\partial \sigma_{BS}} \cdot \ln \dfrac{K_2}{K_1} \cdot \ln \dfrac{K_3}{K_2} \\[2ex]
\dfrac{\partial V^{BS}(t)}{\partial \sigma_{BS}} \cdot \ln \dfrac{K}{K_1} \cdot \ln \dfrac{K}{K_2} \\[2ex]
\dfrac{\partial V_3^{BS}(t)}{\partial \sigma_{BS}} \cdot \ln \dfrac{K_3}{K_1} \cdot \ln \dfrac{K_3}{K_2}
\end{bmatrix}
$$

(3.12)

To differentiate with the empirical price observed in the market, the theoretical value calculated by Vanna-Volga method is referred to as the Vanna-Volga value (V^{VV}), and the Vanna-Volga formula (3.10) is restated as:

$$
V^{VV}(t) = V^{BS}(t) + \sum_{k=1}^{3} w_k(t)\left[V_k^{VV}(t) - V_k^{BS}(t) \right]
$$

(3.13)

The Vanna-Volga formula essentially has a structure similar to that of the TROT valuation formula (2.14). Nevertheless, while the TROT valuation formula limits the correction to a linear combination of 25-Delta risk reversal and 25-Delta butterfly, the Vanna-Volga method extends the choice of correction to any three liquidly traded currency options with same underlying currency and maturity.

The structure of the Vanna-Volga formula (3.13) also suggests that the Vanna-Volga method and the Black-Scholes model share many common characteristics and limitation. For example, the Black-Scholes model assumes that the hedge is conducted in a complete market, that is the variation of the currency option value arising from the currency rate can be hedged with the underlying currency. This assumption of complete market is also applied in the Vanna-Volga method. While the hedging in an incomplete market for the Black-Scholes model is imperfect, such hedging for the Vanna-Volga method is also imperfect. Nevertheless, the limitation of an incomplete market is less critical for both the Black-Scholes model and the Vann-Volga method.

3.1.1.3 Market practices

During the development of the Vanna-Volga method, a latent variable Black-Scholes volatility σ_{BS} has never been specified. Since the ATM currency options are the most liquidly traded in the market, their volatilities are also adopted by traders as the Black-Scholes volatility. In addition, currency option strategies constructed as a linear combination of an ATM currency option, a left 25-Delta Call/Put Option and a right 25-Delta Call/Put Option are also very liquidly traded in the market. Hence, by selecting (i) the ATM volatility as the Black-Scholes volatility, and (ii) a left 25-Delta Call Option, an ATM Call Option and a right 25-Delta Call Option to form the replicating portfolio, that is:

$$\sigma_{BS} = \sigma_{ATM}$$
$$X_1 = \textit{Left 25-Delta Call Option}$$
$$X_2 = \textit{ATM Call Option}$$
$$X_3 = \textit{Right 25-Delta Call Option}$$

$$\sigma_1 = \sigma_{Left\ 25}$$
$$\sigma_2 = \sigma_{ATM}$$
$$\sigma_3 = \sigma_{Right\ 25}$$

$$K_1 = K_{Left\ 25}$$
$$K_2 = K_{ATM}$$
$$K_3 = K_{Right\ 25}$$

$$w_1(t) = w_{Left\ 25}(t)$$
$$w_3(t) = w_{Right\ 25}(t) \tag{3.14}$$

equation (3.13) is simplified into:

$$V^{VV}(t) = V^{BS}(t) + w_{Left\ 25}(t)\left[V^{Market}_{Left\ 25}(t) - V^{BS}_{Left\ 25}(t)\right]$$
$$+ w_{Right\ 25}(t)\left[V^{Market}_{Right\ 25}(t) - V^{BS}_{Right\ 25}(t)\right] \tag{3.15}$$

Therefore, this formula, together with the hedging ratios, provides a simple recipe to valuate the currency option X:

- Collect the left 25-Delta, ATM and right 25-Delta volatilities from financial information providers;
- Use the left 25-Delta and right 25-Delta volatilities to calculate the market prices $V_{Left\ 25}^{Market}(t)$ and $V_{Right\ 25}^{Market}(t)$ of the left 25-Delta Call Option and right 25-Delta Call Option, respectively;
- Use the ATM volatility to calculate the Black-Scholes values $V^{BS}(t)$, $V_{Left\ 25}^{BS}(t)$ and $V_{Right\ 25}^{BS}(t)$ of currency option X, left 25-Delta Call Option and right 25-Delta Call Option, respectively;
- Use equation (3.12) to calculate $w_{Left\ 25}(t)$ and $w_{Right\ 25}(t)$; and
- Use Vanna-Volga formula (3.15) to obtain a Vanna-Volga value of option X.

In contrast to the TROT, the Vanna-Volga method does reproduce values consistent with the market prices of the ATM, left 25-Delta and right 25-Delta Call/Put Options.

3.1.2 Volatility recovery approaches

Given a maturity, the Vanna-Volga method suggests three approaches that can be utilized to recovery the implied volatility of currency option X with only a few market observable parameters by varying the strike rates, resulting in a complete volatility smile. This volatility smile can then be utilized to value other, less liquidly traded vanilla and exotic currency options with the same maturity under the Black-Scholes framework directly.

These approaches are adopted in practice at the trade-off between accuracy and computational efficiency.

3.1.2.1 Root search algorithm

If different strike rates K are substituted into equation (3.15), resulting in different currency option values V^{VV}, which are then put into the Black-Scholes formulas to back out the corresponding implied volatilities with some numerical root search algorithms, a volatility smile is formed. This implicit approach is computationally intensive and less practical since the implied volatility cannot be expressed in a closed-form solution of other variables, thus requiring some numerical methods to search for the root iteratively.

3.1.2.2 Linear approximation

Assume that the correction to Black-Scholes value has arisen from the difference between the implied volatility and the Black-Scholes volatility, then, according to the Taylor series of the first order:

$$V^{VV}(t) \approx V^{BS}(t) + \frac{\partial V^{BS}(t)}{\partial \sigma_{bs}(t)} \cdot \left[\sigma - \sigma_{bs}\right]$$

$$(3.16)$$

From the Vanna-Volga valuation formula (3.13), the correction to Black-Scholes value could also be considered an effect of the differences between the implied volatilities of the three liquidly traded currency options and the Black-Scholes volatility, that is:

$$V^{VV}(t) \approx V^{BS}(t) + \sum_{k=1}^{3} \left\{ w_k(t) \cdot \frac{\partial V_k^{BS}(t)}{\partial \sigma_{BS}(t)} \cdot [\sigma_k - \sigma_{BS}] \right\} \tag{3.17}$$

From equation (3.12)

$$
\begin{bmatrix}
w_1(t) \cdot \dfrac{\partial V_1^{BS}(t)}{\partial \sigma_{BS}} \\[2ex]
w_2(t) \cdot \dfrac{\partial V_2^{BS}(t)}{\partial \sigma_{BS}} \\[2ex]
w_3(t) \cdot \dfrac{\partial V_3^{BS}(t)}{\partial \sigma_{BS}}
\end{bmatrix}
=
\frac{\partial V^{BS}(t)}{\partial \sigma_{BS}}
\begin{bmatrix}
\dfrac{\ln \dfrac{K_2}{K} \cdot \ln \dfrac{K_3}{K}}{\ln \dfrac{K_2}{K_1} \cdot \ln \dfrac{K_3}{K_1}} \\[3ex]
\dfrac{\ln \dfrac{K}{K_1} \cdot \ln \dfrac{K_3}{K}}{\ln \dfrac{K_2}{K_1} \cdot \ln \dfrac{K_3}{K_2}} \\[3ex]
\dfrac{\ln \dfrac{K}{K_1} \cdot \ln \dfrac{K}{K_2}}{\ln \dfrac{K_3}{K_1} \cdot \ln \dfrac{K_3}{K_2}}
\end{bmatrix}
\tag{3.18}
$$

Substituting

$$\frac{\partial V^{BS}(t)}{\partial \sigma_{BS}} = \sum_{k=1}^{3} \left[w_k(t) \cdot \frac{\partial V_k(t)}{\partial \sigma_{BS}} \right] \tag{3.19}$$

equation (3.17) becomes

$$
V^{VV}(t) \approx V^{BS}(t) + \frac{\partial V^{BS}(t)}{\partial \sigma_{BS}}
\begin{bmatrix}
\dfrac{\ln \dfrac{K_2}{K} \cdot \ln \dfrac{K_3}{K}}{\ln \dfrac{K_2}{K_1} \cdot \ln \dfrac{K_3}{K_1}} \sigma_1 + \dfrac{\ln \dfrac{K}{K_1} \cdot \ln \dfrac{K_3}{K}}{\ln \dfrac{K_2}{K_1} \cdot \ln \dfrac{K_3}{K_2}} \sigma_2 \\[4ex]
+ \dfrac{\ln \dfrac{K}{K_1} \cdot \ln \dfrac{K}{K_2}}{\ln \dfrac{K_3}{K_1} \cdot \ln \dfrac{K_3}{K_2}} \sigma_3 - \sigma_{BS}
\end{bmatrix}
\tag{3.20}
$$

Comparing equations (3.17) and (3.20), we can derive the following linear volatility recovery rule:

$$\sigma \approx \frac{\ln \dfrac{K_2}{K} \cdot \ln \dfrac{K_3}{K}}{\ln \dfrac{K_2}{K_1} \cdot \ln \dfrac{K_3}{K_1}} \sigma_1 + \frac{\ln \dfrac{K}{K_1} \cdot \ln \dfrac{K_3}{K}}{\ln \dfrac{K_2}{K_1} \cdot \ln \dfrac{K_3}{K_2}} \sigma_2 + \frac{\ln \dfrac{K}{K_1} \cdot \ln \dfrac{K}{K_2}}{\ln \dfrac{K_3}{K_1} \cdot \ln \dfrac{K_3}{K_2}} \sigma_3$$

(3.21)

This volatility recovery rule essentially states that the implied volatility at strike rate K is the weighted sum of the implied volatilities of the three liquidly traded options, with sum of the weights

$$\frac{\ln \dfrac{K_2}{K} \cdot \ln \dfrac{K_3}{K}}{\ln \dfrac{K_2}{K_1} \cdot \ln \dfrac{K_3}{K_1}} + \frac{\ln \dfrac{K}{K_1} \cdot \ln \dfrac{K_3}{K}}{\ln \dfrac{K_2}{K_1} \cdot \ln \dfrac{K_3}{K_2}} + \frac{\ln \dfrac{K}{K_1} \cdot \ln \dfrac{K}{K_2}}{\ln \dfrac{K_3}{K_1} \cdot \ln \dfrac{K_3}{K_2}} = 1$$

(3.22)

This first-order approximation is a quadratic function of $ln(K)$. Castagna and Mercurio (2007) suggested that this first-order approximation is compatible with the root search algorithm for the strike rates between K_1 and K_3.

3.1.2.3 Quadratic approximation

The accuracy of the linear approximation could be improved by expanding equations (3.16) and (3.17) into a Taylor series of the second order. This results in:

$$V^{VV}(t) \approx V^{BS}(t) + \frac{\partial V^{BS}(t)}{\partial \sigma_{BS}} \cdot (\sigma - \sigma_{bs}) + \frac{1}{2} \frac{\partial^2 V^{BS}(t)}{\partial \sigma_{BS}^2} \cdot (\sigma - \sigma_{bs})^2$$

(3.23)

$$V^{VV}(t) \approx V^{BS}(t) + \sum_{k=1}^{3} \left\{ w_k(t) \left[\begin{array}{l} \dfrac{\partial V_k^{BS}(t)}{\partial \sigma_{BS}(t)} \cdot (\sigma_k - \sigma_{BS}) \\[2mm] + \dfrac{1}{2} \dfrac{\partial^2 V_1^{BS}(t)}{\partial \sigma_{BS}^2(t)} \cdot (\sigma_k - \sigma_{BS})^2 \end{array} \right] \right\}$$

(3.24)

Compare these two second-order formulas and a quadratic equation in this form:

$$C(\sigma - \sigma_{bs})^2 + B(\sigma - \sigma_{bs}) + A = 0$$

(3.25)

where

$$C = \frac{1}{2} \frac{\partial^2 V^{BS}(t)}{\partial \sigma_{BS}^2}$$

$$B = \frac{\partial V^{BS}(t)}{\partial \sigma_{BS}}$$

$$A = -\sum_{k=1}^{3} \left\{ w_k(t) \left[\frac{\partial V_k^{BS}(t)}{\partial \sigma_{BS}(t)} \cdot (\sigma_k - \sigma_{BS}) + \frac{1}{2} \frac{\partial^2 V_k^{BS}(t)}{\partial \sigma_{BS}^2(t)} \cdot (\sigma_k - \sigma_{BS})^2 \right] \right\} \quad (3.26)$$

The general solutions of equation (3.25) are:

$$\sigma = \sigma_2 + \frac{-B + \sqrt{B^2 - 4AC}}{2C} \qquad or$$

$$\sigma = \sigma_2 + \frac{-B - \sqrt{B^2 - 4AC}}{2C} \qquad (3.27)$$

These general solutions may involve three situations:

- When $B^2 - 4AC < 0$, the quadratic approximation breaks down and results in no real solution.
- When $B^2 - 4AC = 0$, there is only one real solution.
- When $B^2 - 4AC > 0$, there are two solutions. Since the formulation of Taylor series assumes that the difference between σ and σ_2 is sufficiently small to ensure the convergence, the solution

$$\sigma = \sigma_2 + \frac{-B + \sqrt{B^2 - 4AC}}{2C}$$

which always results in a smaller difference, is preferred over the solution

$$\sigma = \sigma_2 + \frac{-B - \sqrt{B^2 - 4AC}}{2C}$$

Castagna and Mercurio (2007) suggested that quadratic approximation presented is compatible with root search algorithm even for the strike rates outside the range between K_1 and K_3.

3.2 Assessment methodology

An experiential approach is adopted to assess the performances of the four volatility recovery approaches, namely the Malz formula, linear approximation, quadratic approximation and root search algorithm, under nine scenarios formed by three market conditions against three degrees of moneyness.

For each volatility smile, the ATM, left 25-Delta and right 25-Delta volatilities are adopted as independent variables to recover the volatilities with moneynesses at left/right 35-Delta, 15-Delta and 10-Delta. These recovered volatilities are then compared with the actual volatilities observed from the market. An accurate volatility recovery approach will result in a sufficiently small error most of the time.

Recognizing the fact that this small error is random in nature but governed by some form of probability distribution, a large number of samples are collected under the nine scenarios to determine the domain of application and the overall accuracy of the volatility recovery approaches with hypothesis testing and summary statistics.

3.2.1 Scenarios

The three market conditions are:

- Major currencies: the seven currencies (EUR, GBP, CHF, SEK, CAD, JPY and AUD) with the largest volume of transactions in the international foreign exchange market (BIS, 2012) during the period from 2010 to 2012. This market condition represents the typical situation under which the assumptions of currency option valuation are applicable.
- Stress: the seven currencies with the largest volume of transactions in the international foreign exchange market during the period from June 2008 to July 2009, when the financial tsunami of 2008 hit. This market condition represents situations that deviate from the underlying assumptions of the theory of Vanna-Volga method.
- CNY: the CNY during the period from 2010 to 2012. The CNY is a currency under a government's foreign exchange control and also deviates from the underlying assumptions of the theory of the Vanna-Volga method.

The three degrees of moneyness are:

- Interpolation: the volatilities between the left 25-Delta and the right 25-Delta are recovered;
- Extrapolation: the volatilities with a moderate moneyness outside the left 25-Delta and right 25-Delta are recovered; and
- Extremity: the volatilities with a large moneyness outside the left 25-Delta and right 25-Delta are recovered. This represents an extreme case of extrapolation.

3.2.2 Domain of application

A domain of application is the collection of scenarios under which a volatility recovery approach can be applied to recover volatilities with sufficient accuracy.

This domain of application is quantified by a threshold that is defined as the tolerance level at which a volatility recovery approach starts to fail in delivering recovered volatilities with sufficient accuracy. The lower the threshold, the larger the applicability a volatility recovery approach will be.

There is no universal definition of threshold versus accuracy. In general, a threshold:

- Below 1 percent is considered accurate;
- Between 1 percent and 5 percent is considered adequate;
- Between 5 percent and 10 percent is considered moderate;
- Around 10 percent is considered marginal; and
- Materially above 10 percent is considered inadequate.

Practitioners naturally prefer a stable volatility recovery approach that results in errors that fall within a certain tolerance level most of the time so that practitioners can well prepare for the impact of the model error.

3.2.3 Overall accuracy of volatility recovery approaches

Within the domain of application, the accuracy of a volatility recovery approach is assessed by the average and the standard deviation of the absolute percentage error (APE). A lower average APE suggests that the volatility recovery approach is more accurate in general. In addition, a lower standard deviation of APEs suggests that the volatility recovery approach is more stable in general. Both high accuracy and high stability are preferred characteristics of a volatility recovery approach.

3.2.4 Comparison of volatility recovery approaches

The three volatility recovery approaches are compared in accordance with the domain of application, average APEs and standard deviation of APEs. The Malz formula is selected as the baseline to facilitate the comparison of the volatility recovery approaches derived from the Vanna-Volga method. The Malz formula, linear approximation, quadratic approximation and root search algorithm belong to the same class of volatility recovery approaches without any calibration. Their comparison forms a fair picture of the advantages that might be delivered by the Vanna-Volga method.

3.2.5 Unit of analysis

The unit of analysis is the volatility of the currency rate specified by the underlying currency, maturity, moneyness and transaction date. This volatility is recovered with a volatility recovery approach, and the result is compared with the value observed from the financial market in order to determine its accuracy.

3.2.6 Variables

A recovered volatility is specified by four identification variables and calculated by eight independent variables.

(a) Identification variables

Each recovered volatility is identified by four identification variables:

- Underlying currency: the trading of currency options involves two currencies, a domestic currency in which a transaction is denominated and a foreign currency to which the performance of the currency option is referenced, that is the underlying currency. The USD is selected as the domestic currency since the USD is by far the largest transaction currency in the world, in particular, for currency options. Seven major currencies are selected as foreign currencies. These seven major currencies account for the majority of the transactions in the currency option market (BIS, 2012). In addition, the CNY is also incorporated in the research to study the applicability of the Vanna-Volga method in a currency under foreign exchange control.
- Standard maturity: the standard maturity is the maturity (see independent variables) of a currency option expressed in number of months.
- Moneyness: the moneyness is a measure of how far a strike rate is from the market rate of the underlying currency. The further the strike rate is from the market rate of the underlying currency, the smaller the magnitude of moneyness. In currency option market, moneyness is specified in Delta of a currency option. A Call Option with a low positive Delta or a Put Option with a low negative Delta indicates that the strike rate is far away from the market rate of the underlying currency. In contrast, a Call Option with a moderate positive Delta or a Put Option with a moderate negative Delta indicates that the strike rate is close to the market rate of underlying currency.
- Transaction date: the transaction date is the date on which the day-end closing values of the independent variables are observed.

(b) Independent variables

A recovered volatility is calculated with the following independent variables:

- Market rate of underlying currency: the market rate of underlying currency is the amount of domestic currency required to buy or accepted to sell one unit of foreign currency immediately in the spot market. Since currency options are traded worldwide on a 24/7 basis, the closing prices from the London market are considered the day-end closing price, because London is the largest foreign exchange market in the world.
- Strike rate: the strike rate is the agreed amount of domestic currency required to buy or accepted to sell one unit of foreign currency at the maturity of a currency option.
- ATM volatility: the ATM volatility is the volatility back out from the market price of an ATM currency option by the Black-Scholes formulas.
- Left 25-Delta volatility: the left 25-Delta volatility is backed out from the market price of a Put Option with Delta-25 percent by the Black-Scholes formulas.

- Right 25-Delta volatility: the right 25-Delta volatility is backed out from the market price of a Call Option with Delta 25 percent by the Black-Scholes formulas.
- Domestic risk-free rate: the risk-free rate represents the annualized return that an investor would expect from a risk-free security over a given period of time. In general, the longer the investment horizon, the higher the risk-free rate. Therefore, the risk-free rate is essentially in the form of a term structure instead of a single number. Since USD is selected as the domestic currency, the risk-free rates of USD are adopted as the domestic risk-free rate.
- Foreign risk-free rate: the foreign risk-free rate is the risk-free rate of the foreign currency EUR, GBP, CFH, SEK, CAD, JPY, AUD or CNY selected in this study.
- Maturity: the maturity is the time horizon, measured in years, from today to the expiration date of a currency option. Most currency options traded in the market have maturities of up to one year. In this study, the maturity follows the standard maturities quoted in the market, covering 1 month, 2 months, 3 months, 6 months, 9 months and up to 12 months. Short-dated currency options are excluded to eliminate the potential impacts of public holidays, and long-dated currency options are excluded because of their low transaction volumes.

(c) Dependent variable

Throughout this study, there is only one dependent variable:

- Recovered volatility: the recovered volatility is the volatility calculated by a volatility recovery approach.

3.2.7 Measurement

The accuracy of a recovered volatility is assessed by how far it deviates from the corresponding value observed from the financial market.

In this study, the absolute percentage error (APE) of a recovered volatility, defined as

$$\left| \frac{Volatility\ calculated\ with\ a\ volatility\ recovery\ approach}{Volatility\ observed\ actually\ from\ the\ market} - 1 \right| \cdot 100\%$$

is adopted as the measurement of the accuracy of recovered volatility. The APE has the advantages that it:

- Takes into account only the magnitude of the error and avoids overestimations and underestimations to offset with one another when the summary statistics are calculated;
- Recognizes the practice of accepting a higher tolerance in terms of magnitude for a larger volatility.

3.2.8 Sample selection

The specifications of the samples selected for the analysis are set out in Table 3.1. The major currency analysis comprises seven major currencies, six standard maturities, six moneynesses and 157 Fridays, a total of 39,564 samples. The stress analysis comprises seven major currencies, six standard maturities, six moneynesses and 52 Fridays, a total of 13,014 samples. The CNY analysis comprises the CNY, six standard maturities, six moneynesses and 157 Fridays, a total of 5,652 samples.

3.2.9 Data analysis

The data analysis is divided into two stages. In the first stage, for each scenario, a binomial test is conducted to assess at which range a volatility recovery approach will recover a volatility smile with sufficient accuracy. Subject to the 95 percent confidence level, 1 percent probability and number of samples, a critical value for the binomial test is calculated from a binomial distribution. If the number of samples with an APE above the tolerance level is greater than this critical level, it is

Table 3.1 Sample selection

(A) Major currencies analysis

Test	Interpolation	Extrapolation	Extremity
Currency	EUR, GBP, CHF, SEK, CAD, JPY, AUD		
Standard maturity	1, 2, 3, 6, 9 and 12 months		
Moneyness	Left and right 35-Delta	Left and right 15-Delta	Left and right 10-Delta
Date	157 Fridays during the period from 2010 to 2012		
No. of samples	39,564		

(B) Stress analysis

Test	Interpolation	Extrapolation	Extremity
Currency	EUR, GBP, CHF, SEK, CAD, JPY, AUD		
Standard maturity	1, 2, 3, 6, 9 and 12 months		
Moneyness	Left and right 35-Delta	Left and right 15-Delta	Left and right 10-Delta
Date	52 Fridays during the period from July 2008 to June 2009		
No. of samples	13,014		

(C) CNY analysis

Test	Interpolation	Extrapolation	Extremity
Currency	CNY		
Standard maturity	1, 2, 3, 6, 9 and 12 months		
Moneyness	Left and right 35-Delta	Left and right 15-Delta	Left and right 10-Delta
Date	157 Fridays during the period from 2010 to 2012		
No. of samples	5,652		

concluded that volatilities are not recovered at an accuracy matching the tolerance level. A number of tolerance levels are set out, and the binomial tests are repeated against these tolerance levels. A threshold is the tolerance level at which a volatility recovery approach starts to produce too many samples with APEs above that particular tolerance level. This threshold defines the domain of application of a volatility recovery approach. Within the domain of application, the high accuracy of the volatilities calculated by a volatility recovery approach guarantees the usefulness of the recovered volatilities. Outside the domain of application, the lower accuracy of the volatilities calculated by a volatility recovery approach makes the application less applicable.

The second stage of data analysis seeks to compare the relative performances of the volatility recovery approaches by contrasting the summary statistics of the APEs. For each scenario within the domain of application, the average and the standard deviation of the APEs are calculated and compared with those calculated for the different volatility recovery approaches. While the average of the APEs suggests the overall magnitude of the errors, the standard deviation of the APEs indicates the stability of the errors. As such, a volatility recovery approach with a small APE average and standard deviation is preferred.

3.2.10 Hypothesis construction

To test the accuracy of recovered volatilities with regard to a selected tolerance level, a binomial test at the 95 percent confidence level is proposed:

$H1_0$: Probability[APE of recovered volatility > tolerance level] < 1%

$H1_a$: Probability[APE of recovered volatility > tolerance level] > 1%

A critical value is calculated in accordance with the binomial distribution with respect to the 95 percent confidence level and a 1 percent probability. If the null hypothesis is rejected, with the number of samples with APE over the tolerance level above the critical value, then the recovered volatilities should not be considered accurate with respect to that tolerance level.

3.3 Results and discussions

This section summarizes the testing results for the performance of the Malz formula, linear approximation, quadratic approximation and root search algorithm in terms of summary statistics and binomial tests under three groups of scenarios.

3.3.1 Major currency analysis

The summary statistics and binomial testing results for the Malz formula, linear approximation, quadratic approximation and root search algorithm are exhibited in Tables 3.2, 3.3 and 3.4, respectively. The corresponding graphical comparisons are also illustrated in Figures 3.1, 3.2 and 3.3, respectively.

In general, the performances of the volatility recovery approaches, in terms of the average of the APEs, standard deviation of the APEs and number of samples with the APE above a certain tolerance level, deteriorate with a decreasing magnitude of moneyness and improve with an increasing level of sophistication (the complexity of implementation).

The quadratic approximation tracks closely and outperforms slightly the accuracy of root search algorithm. The Malz formula and the linear approach occupy the worst and second-worst positions under different scenarios.

When the volatility recovery approaches are utilized for interpolating a volatility smile, at a confidence level of 95 percent, the null hypothesis is rejected for:

- The Malz formula at the 0.9 percent tolerance level;
- Linear approximation at the 0.7 percent tolerance level;
- Quadratic approximation at the 0.6 percent tolerance level; and
- Root search algorithm at the 0.6 percent tolerance level.

The hypothesis testing suggests that the four approaches demonstrate a high degree of accuracy when interpolating a volatility smile. There is a small marginal benefit in the improvement of the accuracy in response to the level of sophistication.

When the volatility recovery approaches are utilized for extrapolating a volatility smile at a moderate moneyness, at a confidence level of 95 percent, the null hypothesis is rejected for:

- The Malz formula at the 4 percent tolerance level;
- Linear approximation at the 4 percent tolerance level;
- Quadratic approximation at the 3 percent tolerance level; and
- Root search algorithm at the 3 percent tolerance level.

The hypothesis testing suggests that the four approaches demonstrate an adequate degree of accuracy when extrapolating a volatility smile at a moderate moneyness. They exhibit a similar degree of deterioration as a result of the decreasing degree of moneyness.

When the volatility recovery approaches are utilized for extrapolating the volatility smile at an extreme moneyness, at a confidence level of 95 percent, the null hypothesis is rejected for:

- The Malz formula at the 8 percent tolerance level;
- Linear approximation at the 10 percent tolerance level;
- Quadratic approximation at the 6 percent tolerance level; and
- Root search algorithm at the 6 percent tolerance level.

The Malz formula, quadratic approximation and root search algorithm demonstrate a moderate degree of accuracy for extrapolating volatility smile at an extreme moneyness. The performance of linear approximation deteriorates significantly with the decreasing degree of moneyness.

Table 3.2 Summary statistics and binomial testing results under the major currency, interpolation scenarios

Type of analysis	Major currencies		

Type of volatility recovery	Interpolation		

Summary statistics

(%)	Malz formula	Linear approximation	Quadratic approximation	Root search algorithm
Average	0.3381	0.1588	0.1240	0.1269
Std. dev.	0.2031	0.1546	0.1293	0.1327
Minimum	0.0001	0.0000	0.0000	0.0000
Maximum	1.2850	1.5068	1.2532	1.2787
Binomial test				
Confidence level		95%		
Probability of the APE below tolerance level		1%		
Number of samples		13,188		
Critical value		151		

Tolerance level	No. of samples with the APE above the tolerance level			
(%)	Malz formula	Linear approximation	Quadratic approximation	Root search algorithm
0.1	11,771*	7,534*	5,945*	6,084*
0.2	9,691*	3,654*	2,199*	2,280*
0.3	6,838*	1,650*	954*	992*
0.4	4,335*	798*	543*	569*
0.5	2,594*	457*	340*	359*
0.6	1,473*	309*	208*	226*
0.7	735*	220*	119	140
0.8	387*	135	62	78
0.9	166*	65	25	32
1	54	39	6	11
2	0	0	0	0
3	0	0	0	0
4	0	0	0	0
5	0	0	0	0
6	0	0	0	0
7	0	0	0	0
8	0	0	0	0
9	0	0	0	0
10	0	0	0	0
*	Null hypothesis rejected			

Table 3.3 Summary statistics and binomial testing results under the major currency, extrapolation scenarios

Type of analysis	Major currencies		
Type of volatility recovery	*Extrapolation*		
Summary statistics			

(%)	Malz formula	Linear approximation	Quadratic approximation	Root search algorithm
Average	1.3689	1.5620	0.7487	0.7670
Std. dev.	1.0380	1.1957	0.7499	0.7515
Minimum	0.0001	0.0000	0.0000	0.0000
Maximum	8.7966	10.9056	8.3596	8.6440
Binomial test				
Confidence level			95%	
Probability of the APE below tolerance level			1%	
Number of samples			13,188	
Critical value			151	

Tolerance level	*No. of samples with the APE above the tolerance level*			
(%)	Malz formula	Linear approximation	Quadratic approximation	Root search algorithm
0.1	12,495*	12,469*	11,771*	11,863*
0.2	11,888*	11,884*	10,435*	10,656*
0.3	11,262*	11,310*	9,163*	9,493*
0.4	10,676*	10,772*	7,947*	8,325*
0.5	10,162*	10,281*	6,810*	7,184*
0.6	9,634*	9,811*	5,847*	6,165*
0.7	9,074*	9,386*	5,057*	5,300*
0.8	8,519*	9,009*	4,381*	4,601*
0.9	8,003*	8,617*	3,775*	3,935*
1	7,442*	8,234*	3,290*	3,350*
2	3,201*	4,075*	911*	863*
3	967*	1,572*	281*	315*
4	280*	503*	80	95
5	83	145	9	15
6	11	57	3	3
7	1	29	1	2
8	1	6	1	1
9	0	4	0	0
10	0	2	0	0
*	Null hypothesis rejected			

Table 3.4 Summary statistics and binomial testing results under the major currency, extremity scenarios

Type of analysis			Major currencies	
Type of volatility recovery			Extremity	

Summary statistics

(%)	Malz formula	Linear approximation	Quadratic approximation	Root search algorithm
Average	2.7162	3.6602	1.4290	1.4417
Std. dev.	1.8961	2.9246	1.4509	1.4780
Minimum	0.0001	0.0010	0.0000	0.0002
Maximum	14.1358	24.7384	15.2485	15.9559
Binomial test				
Confidence level			95%	
Probability of the APE below tolerance level			1%	
Number of samples			13,188	
Critical value			151	

Tolerance level	No. of samples with the APE above the tolerance level			

(%)	Malz formula	Linear approximation	Quadratic approximation	Root search algorithm
0.1	12,884*	12,885*	12,469*	12,532*
0.2	12,552*	12,610*	11,780*	11,860*
0.3	12,282*	12,298*	11,037*	11,156*
0.4	12,000*	11,980*	10,358*	10,504*
0.5	11,696*	11,680*	9,582*	9,772*
0.6	11,424*	11,367*	8,835*	8,989*
0.7	11,121*	11,050*	8,190*	8,251*
0.8	10,837*	10,754*	7,507*	7,545*
0.9	10,582*	10,496*	6,888*	6,866*
1	10,325*	10,220*	6,355*	6,276*
2	7,690*	8,360*	3,011*	3,001*
3	5,331*	7,041*	1,563*	1,586*
4	3,242*	5,423*	921*	940*
5	1,546*	3,763*	507*	515*
6	744*	2,510*	229*	269*
7	333*	1,698*	116	138
8	154*	1,084*	44	61
9	62	674*	12	19
10	18	429*	5	7
	Null hypothesis rejected			

In summary, for a major currency at a regular market, both the quadratic approximation approach and root search algorithm perform equally well for the recovery of the volatility smile, although root search algorithm is more sophisticated than quadratic approximation. The Malz formula serves as an adequate alternative only if the moneyness is readily quoted in Delta. It comes with a much simpler implementation at a slightly lower performance. The Malz formula, quadratic approximation and root search algorithm are subject to an acceptable tolerance level most of the time, even at the extremities of a volatility smile.

No. of samples with the APE above tolerance level

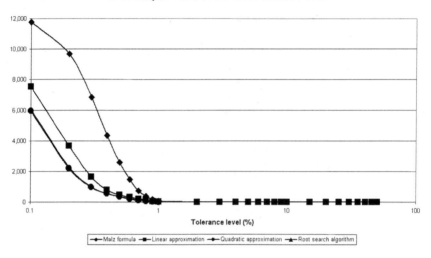

Figure 3.1 Performance comparison for the major currencies, interpolation scenarios

No. of samples with the APE above tolerance level

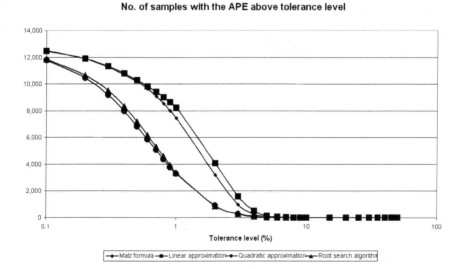

Figure 3.2 Performance comparison for the major currencies, extrapolation scenarios

No. of samples with the APE above tolerance level

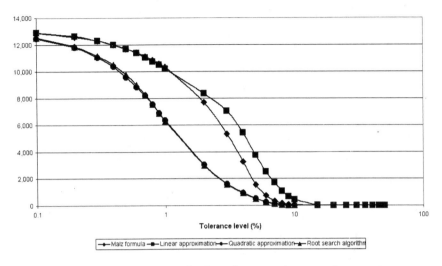

Figure 3.3 Performance comparison for the major currencies, extremity scenarios

3.3.2 Stress analysis

The summary statistics and binomial testing results for the Malz formula, linear approximation, quadratic approximation and root search algorithm are exhibited in Tables 3.5, 3.6 and 3.7, respectively. The corresponding graphical comparisons are also illustrated in Figures 3.4, 3.5 and 3.6, respectively.

In general, the performances of the volatility recovery approaches, in terms of the number of samples with the APE above a certain tolerance level, deteriorate with an increasing level of sophistication and a decreasing degree of moneyness. There is no conclusive observation in terms of the average of APEs and standard deviation of the APEs.

When interpolating a volatility smile, the four volatility recovery approaches perform similarly, in terms of the average of the APEs, standard deviation of the APEs and number of samples with the APE above a certain tolerance level. When extrapolating the volatility smile, the Malz formula outperforms the rest in terms of the number of samples with the APE above a certain tolerance level.

When the volatility recovery approaches are utilized for interpolating the volatility smile, at a confidence level of 95 percent, the null hypothesis is rejected for the Malz formula, linear approximation, quadratic approximation and root search algorithm, all at the 1 percent tolerance level.

The hypothesis testing suggests that the four approaches demonstrate a similar and adequate degree of accuracy when interpolating a volatility smile. There is no marginal benefit in the improvement of the accuracy in response to the level of sophistication.

Table 3.5 Summary statistics and binomial testing results under the major currency, interpolation scenarios

Type of analysis	Stress

Type of volatility recovery	Interpolation

Summary statistics

(%)	Malz formula	Linear approximation	Quadratic approximation	Root search algorithm
Average	0.3551	0.3151	0.3302	0.3283
Std. dev.	0.4356	0.3594	0.4080	0.4031
Minimum	0.0000	0.0001	0.0001	0.0000
Maximum	3.7377	4.9470	5.2088	5.4061

Binomial test

Confidence level	95%
Probability of the APE below tolerance level	1%
Number of samples	4,368
Critical value	55

Tolerance level	No. of samples with the APE above the tolerance level			
(%)	Malz formula	Linear approximation	Quadratic approximation	Root search algorithm
0.5	827*	817*	810*	811*
0.6	641*	629*	654*	654*
0.7	527*	501*	549*	552*
0.8	452*	394*	463*	458*
0.9	400*	291*	383*	377*
1	347*	218*	320*	299*
2	55	23	43	37
3	3	3	4	4
4	0	2	3	3
5	0	0	1	1
6	0	0	0	0
7	0	0	0	0
8	0	0	0	0
9	0	0	0	0
10	0	0	0	0
15	0	0	0	0
20	0	0	0	0
25	0	0	0	0
*	Null hypothesis rejected			

Table 3.6 Summary statistics and binomial testing results under stress, extrapolation scenarios

Type of analysis			Stress	

Type of volatility recovery			Extrapolation	

Summary statistics

(%)	Malz formula	Linear approximation	Quadratic approximation	Root search algorithm
Average	1.7709	1.3791	1.3899	1.4467
Std. dev.	1.2770	1.5944	2.3139	2.5293
Minimum	0.0034	0.0005	0.0003	0.0007
Maximum	8.2922	14.3698	19.0704	25.4787

Binomial test

Confidence level	95%
Probability of the APE below tolerance level	1%
Number of samples	4,368
Critical value	55

Tolerance level	No. of samples with the APE above the tolerance level			
(%)	Malz formula	Linear approximation	Quadratic approximation	Root search algorithm
0.5	3,968*	3,148*	2,435*	2,486*
0.6	3,862*	2,919*	2,127*	2,182*
0.7	3,729*	2,692*	1,821*	1,894*
0.8	3,560*	2,492*	1,579*	1,653*
0.9	3,380*	2,263*	1,385*	1,445*
1	3,196*	2,065*	1,222*	1,282*
2	1,276*	853*	710*	696*
3	536*	367*	560*	560*
4	317*	236*	447*	444*
5	166*	175*	352*	349*
6	61*	131*	270*	265*
7	24	85*	212*	209*
8	6	56*	153*	168*
9	0	37	106*	134*
10	0	22	75*	99*
15	0	0	8	25
20	0	0	0	3
25	0	0	0	1
*	Null hypothesis rejected			

Table 3.7 Summary statistics and binomial testing results under stress, extremity scenarios

Type of analysis			Stress	
Type of volatility recovery			Extremity	

Summary statistics

(%)	Malz formula	Linear approximation	Quadratic approximation	Root search algorithm
Average	3.7700	3.4964	3.1610	2.8741
Std. dev.	2.5887	3.7943	6.4997	5.5931
Minimum	0.0009	0.0019	0.0012	0.0009
Maximum	18.0240	43.5253	84.1218	55.6408

Binomial test

Confidence level	95%
Probability of the APE below tolerance level	1%
Number of samples	4,368
Critical value	55

Tolerance level	No. of samples with the APE above the tolerance level			
(%)	Malz formula	Linear approximation	Quadratic approximation	Root search algorithm
1	3,991*	3,634*	2,088*	2,254*
2	3,340*	2,703*	993*	974*
3	2,485*	1,825*	801*	764*
4	1,584*	1,193*	718*	670*
5	935*	777*	646*	597*
6	561*	529*	583*	533*
7	382*	369*	525*	461*
8	296*	287*	479*	422*
9	227*	245*	450*	392*
10	172*	214*	427*	365*
15	11	116*	255*	211*
20	0	52	157*	126*
25	0	17	93*	72*
30	0	6	54	37
35	0	3	37	25
40	0	1	20	9
45	0	0	12	1
50	0	0	6	1
*	Null hypothesis rejected			

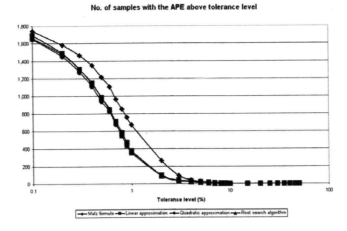

Figure 3.4 Performance comparison for stress, interpolation scenarios

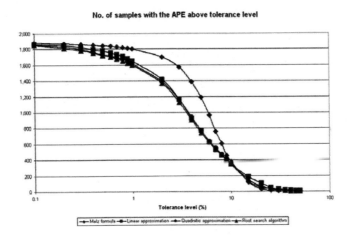

Figure 3.5 Performance comparison for stress, extrapolation scenarios

When the volatility recovery approaches are utilized for extrapolating the volatility smile at a moderate moneyness, at a confidence level of 95 percent, the null hypothesis is rejected for:

- The Malz formula at the 6 percent tolerance level;
- Linear approximation at the 8 percent tolerance level;
- Quadratic approximation at the 10 percent tolerance level; and
- Root search algorithm at the 10 percent tolerance level.

The Malz formula and linear approximation demonstrate a moderate degree of accuracy when the volatility smile is being extrapolated. Quadratic approximation

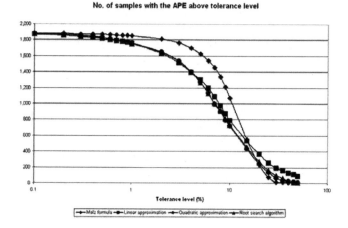

Figure 3.6 Performance comparison for stress, extremity scenarios

and root search algorithm demonstrate a marginal level of accuracy when the volatilities are being extrapolated.

When the volatility recovery approaches are utilized for extrapolating the volatility smile at an extreme moneyness at a confidence level of 95 percent, the null hypothesis is rejected for:

• The Malz formula at the 10 percent tolerance level;
• Linear approximation at the 15 percent tolerance level;
• Quadratic approximation at the 25 percent tolerance level; and
• Root search algorithm at the 25 percent tolerance level.

Only the Malz formula exhibits a margin level of accuracy. Other volatility recovery approaches deliver an unacceptable accuracy.

In summary, for a major currency in a stress market, the Malz formula appears to be the best approach for the recovery of volatility smile. This observation is explained by the difference between the underlying theories of model construction. While the Malz formula is purely a numerical curve fitting technique, the Vanna-Volga method follows all assumptions of the Black-Scholes framework and the dynamic portfolio replication, which are less applicable under a stress market condition.

3.3.3 CNY analysis

The summary statistics and binomial testing results for the Malz formula, linear approximation, quadratic approximation and root search algorithm are exhibited in Tables 3.8, 3.9 and 3.10, respectively. The corresponding graphical comparisons are also illustrated in Figures 3.7, 3.8 and 3.9, respectively.

Table 3.8 Summary statistics and binomial testing results under the CNY, interpolation scenarios

Type of analysis			CNY	
Type of volatility recovery			Interpolation	

Summary statistics

(%)	Malz formula	Linear approximation	Quadratic approximation	Root search algorithm
Average	1.0319	0.7359	0.7025	0.7023
Std. dev.	1.0796	0.9453	0.8801	0.8376
Minimum	0.0028	0.0019	0.0004	0.0003
Maximum	9.1593	11.9003	14.1939	12.9851

Binomial test

Confidence level	95%
Probability of the APE below tolerance level	1%
Number of samples	1,884
Critical value	26

Tolerance level — *No. of samples with the APE above the tolerance level*

(%)	Malz formula	Linear approximation	Quadratic approximation	Root search algorithm
1	672*	377*	352*	355*
2	262*	96*	90*	89*
3	93*	39*	36*	34*
4	40*	29*	19	19
5	23	21	13	14
6	15	15	10	7
7	9	8	7	3
8	5	6	4	2
9	1	5	3	2
10	0	2	2	2
15	0	0	0	0
20	0	0	0	0
25	0	0	0	0
30	0	0	0	0
35	0	0	0	0
40	0	0	0	0
45	0	0	0	0
50	0	0	0	0
*	Null hypothesis rejected			

Table 3.9 Summary statistics and binomial testing results under the CNY, extrapolation scenarios

Type of analysis	CNY

Type of volatility recovery	Extrapolation

Summary statistics

(%)	Malz formula	Linear approximation	Quadratic approximation	Root search algorithm
Average	7.0231	6.3542	5.8871	5.8601
Std. dev.	5.1165	7.4432	6.3352	6.1837
Minimum	0.0095	0.0007	0.0021	0.0056
Maximum	58.7581	72.6594	75.3785	42.9735

Binomial test

Confidence level	95%
Probability of the APE below tolerance level	1%
Number of samples	1,884
Critical value	26

Tolerance level	No. of samples with the APE above the tolerance level			
(%)	Malz formula	Linear approximation	Quadratic approximation	Root search algorithm
1	1,803*	1,648*	1,619*	1,600*
2	1,696*	1,417*	1,387*	1,371*
3	1,573*	1,163*	1,164*	1,125*
4	1,389*	923*	938*	905*
5	1,188*	770*	769*	738*
6	963*	620*	631*	624*
7	758*	527*	548*	543*
8	607*	458*	464*	462*
9	457*	401*	413*	406*
10	377*	346*	347*	355*
15	116*	183*	127*	147*
20	31*	102*	51*	63*
25	14	47*	30*	35*
30	10	27*	15	22
35	7	19	13	12
40	7	14	7	4
45	5	11	6	0
50	4	8	5	0
*	Null hypothesis rejected			

Table 3.10 Summary statistics and binomial testing results under the CNY, extremity scenarios

Type of analysis	CNY
Type of volatility recovery	Extremity

Summary statistics

(%)	Malz formula	Linear approximation	Quadratic approximation	Root search algorithm
Average	12.1247	13.5195	10.2829	10.5966
Std. dev.	7.1484	16.4141	9.4483	9.5746
Minimum	0.0091	0.0053	0.0106	0.0000
Maximum	76.0455	173.1354	126.5096	56.1373

Binomial test

Confidence level	95%
Probability of the APE below tolerance level	1%
Number of samples	1,884
Critical value	26

Tolerance level	No. of samples with the APE above the tolerance level			
(%)	Malz formula	Linear approximation	Quadratic approximation	Root search algorithm
1	1,850*	1,758*	1,762*	1,753*
2	1,813*	1,631*	1,647*	1,613*
3	1,763*	1,512*	1,537*	1,531*
4	1,700*	1,395*	1,400*	1,398*
5	1,625*	1,300*	1,271*	1,267*
6	1,541*	1,197*	1,135*	1,131*
7	1,453*	1,089*	994*	1,005*
8	1,340*	975*	900*	912*
9	1,210*	876*	792*	812*
10	1,070*	788*	719*	731*
15	548*	531*	438*	457*
20	236*	368*	245*	273*
25	78*	259*	139*	163*
30	15	194*	68*	101*
35	12	160*	38*	62*
40	10	130*	27*	31*
45	9	111*	18	15
50	7	88*	10	9
*	Null hypothesis rejected			

No. of samples with the APE above tolerance level

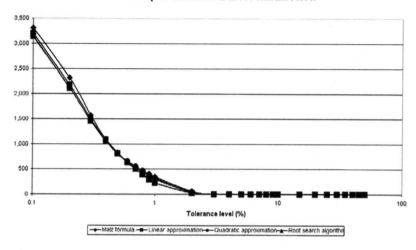

Figure 3.7 Performance comparison for the CNY, interpolation scenarios

No. of samples with the APE above tolerance level

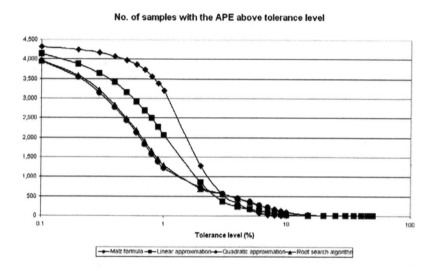

Figure 3.8 Performance comparison for the CNY, extrapolation scenarios

In general, the performance of volatility recovery approaches, in terms of the average of the APEs, standard deviation of the APEs and number of samples with the APE above a certain tolerance level, deteriorates with a decreasing degree of moneyness and an increasing level of sophistication.

When interpolating the volatility smile, the four volatility recovery approaches perform similarly. When extrapolating the volatility smile, none of the volatility recovery approaches delivers an acceptable accuracy.

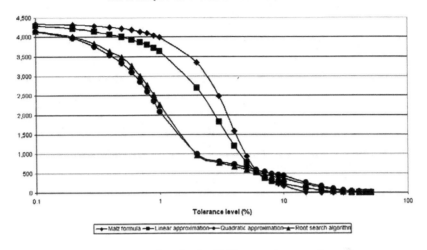

Figure 3.9 Performance comparison for the CNY, extremity scenarios

When the volatility recovery approaches are utilized for interpolating the volatility smile at a confidence level of 95 percent, the null hypothesis is rejected for:

- The Malz formula at the 4 percent tolerance level;
- Linear approximation at the 4 percent tolerance level;
- Quadratic approximation at the 3 percent tolerance level; and
- Root search algorithm at the 3 percent tolerance level.

The hypothesis testing suggests that the four approaches demonstrate a similar and adequate degree of accuracy when interpolating the volatility smile. There is a small marginal benefit on the improvement of the accuracy with respect to the level of sophistication.

When the volatility recovery approaches are utilized for extrapolating the volatility smile at a moderate moneyness at a confidence level of 95 percent, the null hypothesis is rejected for:

- The Malz formula at the 20 percent tolerance level;
- Linear approximation at the 30 percent tolerance level;
- Quadratic approximation at the 30 percent tolerance level; and
- Root search algorithm at the 25 percent tolerance level.

None of the volatility recovery approaches delivers an acceptable accuracy.

When the volatility recovery approaches are utilized for extrapolating the volatility smile at an extreme moneyness at a confidence level of 95 percent, the null hypothesis is rejected for:

- The Malz formula at the 25 percent tolerance level;
- Linear approximation at the 50 percent tolerance level;

- Quadratic approximation at the 40 percent tolerance level; and
- Root search algorithm at the 40 percent tolerance level.

Again, none of the volatility recovery approaches delivers an acceptable accuracy.

In summary, for the CNY at a regular market, when interpolating a volatility smile, the volatility recovery approaches revert to a generic curve fitting technique, and when used for extrapolating a volatility smile, the theories of both the Malz formula and the Vanna-Volga method break down completely.

3.3.4 Domain of application

The Malz formula and the three Vanna-Volga method–based approaches share the same domain of application. Both families deliver a performance within the same order of magnitude at:

- An adequate accuracy when (i) interpolating a volatility smile, and (ii) extrapolating a volatility smile for a major currency at a regular market and a moderate moneyness;
- A marginal accuracy when extrapolating a volatility for a major currency at (i) a regular market and extreme moneyness, and (ii) a stress market and moderate moneyness; and
- A failure in extrapolating a volatility smile for (i) a major currency at a regular market at an extreme moneyness, and (ii) the CNY.

The Adequate and Marginal zones in Table 3.11 form the domain of application for the four volatility recovery approaches.

Table 3.12 exhibits the summary statistics of the four volatility recovery approaches within the domain of application.

Within the domain of application, linear approximation performs well when interpolating a volatility smile. Statistically, linear approximation outperforms the Malz formula in all three interpolation scenarios and underperforms consistently quadratic approximation and root search algorithm in two of the three interpolation scenarios.

Both quadratic approximation and root search algorithm outperform significantly the Malz formula in four out of six scenarios, perform comparably to the

Table 3.11 Domain of application

	Interpolation	*Extrapolation*	*Extremity*
Major currency	Adequate	Adequate	Marginal
Stress	Adequate	Marginal	**Failed**
CNY	Adequate	**Failed**	**Failed**

Table 3.12 Summary statistics within the domain of application

		Malz formula	*Linear approximation*	*Quadratic approximation*	*Root search algorithm*
Normal currency — Interpolation	**Threshold (%)**	0.9	0.7	0.6	
	Average (%)	0.3381	0.1588	0.1240	0.1269
	Std. dev. (%)	0.2031	0.1546	0.1293	0.1327
	t-statistic	191	118	110	110
Normal currency — Extrapolation	**Threshold (%)**	4	4	3	
	Average (%)	1.3689	1.5620	0.7487	0.7670
	Std. dev. (%)	1.0380	1.1957	0.7499	0.7515
	t-statistic	151	150	115	117
Stress — Extremity	**Threshold (%)**	8	10	6	
	Average (%)	2.7162	3.6602	1.4290	1.4417
	Std. dev. (%)	1.8961	2.9246	1.4509	1.4780
	t-statistic	165	144	113	112
Stress — Interpolation	**Threshold (%)**	1	1	1	
	Average (%)	0.3551	0.3151	0.3302	0.3283
	Std. dev. (%)	0.4356	0.3594	0.4080	0.4031
	t-statistic	54	58	53	54
Stress — Extrapolation	**Threshold (%)**	6	8	10	
	Average (%)	1.7709	1.3791	1.3899	1.4467
	Std. dev. (%)	1.2770	1.5944	2.3139	2.5293
	t-statistic	92	57	40	38
CNY — Interpolation	**Threshold (%)**	4	4	3	
	Average (%)	1.0319	0.7359	0.7025	0.7023
	Std. dev. (%)	1.0796	0.9453	0.8801	0.8376
	t-statistic	41	34	35	36

Malz formula in one interpolation scenario and underperform the Malz formula in one extrapolation scenario. Although the reduction in the threshold is less material, the APEs of the four outperformed scenarios have significantly lower averages, standard deviations and t-statistics than do those of the Malz formula.

Quadratic approximation tracks closely the performance of the root search algorithm in all scenarios. Both approaches have the same thresholds within the domain of application and very close APE averages, standard deviations and t-statistics. Taking into account its simpler implementation, quadratic approximation serves as the best choice of implementation among the four volatility recovery approaches.

3.4 Conclusions

An empirical study of the performance of the volatility recovery approaches derived from the Vanna-Volga method is conducted, with the Malz formula as a baseline reference. The binomial test is adopted to assess the performance of these volatility recovery approaches in order to identify the domain of application, in addition to the relative accuracy, of various approaches.

The study demonstrates that the Malz formula, linear approximation, quadratic approximation and root search algorithm have the same domain of application, primary because of the shared underlying theory of geometric Brownian motion in currency rates.

Within the domain of application, in general, quadratic approximation and root search algorithm outperform the Malz formula and linear approximation. When interpolating a volatility smile, all the volatility recovery approaches result in volatilities with similar accuracy, and quadratic approximation and root search algorithm add only a small marginal benefit. When extrapolating a volatility smile, the performance of quadratic approximation and root search algorithm is superior to that of the Malz formula and linear approximation.

The performances of the volatility recovery approaches deteriorate with a decreasing degree of moneyness. In other words, when the strike rate is close to the spot currency rate, the volatility recovery approaches deliver quite accurate results. When the strike rate is either materially below or above the spot currency rate, the volatility recovery approaches deliver less satisfactory results.

When recovering a volatility smile, they work well for a major currency in a regular market, moderately for a major currency in a stress market and marginally for the CNY.

Quadratic approximation tracks closely the performance of root search algorithm. Taking into account its simplicity of implementation, the quadratic approximation serves as the best choice among the four volatility recovery approaches.

4 Value-at-risk calculation

Quadratic approximation has been demonstrated in Chapter 3 to be an effective volatility recovery method that can be implemented analytically in closed-form solution with only a few input parameters readily available from major financial information providers. This chapter studies the performance of measuring the market risk of currency options with the one-day VaR amount at the 99th percentile confidence level using the Delta-Gamma VaR approach, riding on the volatility derived from quadratic approximation.

4.1 Theoretical framework

The theoretical framework comprises:

- The analytical calculation of one-day VaR amount using Delta-Gamma approximation with noncentral Chi-squared distribution in closed-form solution; and
- The statistical assessment of the accuracy of this VaR methodology using the Kupiec-Lopez test.

The theory starts with the assumptions that:

- Volatility is calculated with sufficient accuracy by quadratic approximation of the Vanna-Volga method studied in Chapter 3. This facilitates the development of the relevant theories in accordance with the Black-Scholes framework and derivation of the closed-form solution for one-day VaR amount calculation;
- The market rate of underlying currency dominates the market risk of a currency option; and
- The daily drifts of the currency rates are independent random numbers following a normal distribution.

4.1.1 Delta-Gamma noncentral Chi-squared VaR methodology

Since the Delta-normal VaR methodology described in Chapter 2 ignores the effects of the higher-order terms in the Taylor series, the methodology tends to overestimate the one-day VaR amount for a long position in a currency option. To address this issue and improve the accuracy, the second-order term in the Taylor series is included in the approximation of the change in currency option value arising from a small change in the underlying currency rate in order to incorporate the curvature effect. This results in:

$$dV\left[S(t)\right] \approx Delta \cdot dS(t) + \frac{Gamma}{2} \cdot \left[dS(t)\right]^2$$

$$= Delta \cdot S(t) \cdot \frac{dS(t)}{S(t)} + \frac{Gamma}{2} \cdot \left[S(t)\right]^2 \cdot \left[\frac{dS(t)}{S(t)}\right]^2$$

$$= \frac{Gamma}{2} \cdot \left[S(t)\right]^2 \cdot \left\{SD\left[\frac{dS(t)}{S(t)}\right]\right\}^2$$

$$\cdot \left\{ \frac{\frac{dS(t)}{S(t)} + \frac{Delta}{Gamma \cdot S(t)}}{SD\left[\frac{dS(t)}{S(t)}\right]} \right\}^2 - \frac{Delta^2}{2Gamma}$$

(4.1)

Since the daily drift of currency rate $\frac{dS(t)}{S(t)}$ follows a normal distribution, the

term $\left\{ \frac{\frac{dS(t)}{S(t)} + \frac{Delta}{Gamma \cdot S(t)}}{SD\left[\frac{dS(t)}{S(t)}\right]} \right\}^2$ essentially follows a noncentral Chi-squared

distribution with one degree of freedom and noncentrality parameter

$\left\{ \frac{\frac{Delta}{Gamma \cdot S(t)}}{SD\left[\frac{dS(t)}{S(t)}\right]} \right\}^2$. Given a confidence level, the corresponding quantile of the

noncentral Chi-squared distribution can be derived with some numerical methods or analytical approximations.

For a long position in a currency option, the Gamma is always positive. Therefore, when $dV(t)$ is at the 99th percentile confidence level, the term

$\left\{ \frac{\frac{dS(t)}{S(t)} + \frac{Delta}{Gamma \cdot S(t)}}{SD\left[\frac{dS(t)}{S(t)}\right]} \right\}^2$ is at the 1st percentile confidence level.

Sankaran (1963) derived in his early paper a simple closed-form approximation of the cumulative noncentral Chi-squared distribution function. Given the degree of freedom k and the noncentrality parameter λ, the cumulative noncentral Chi-squared distribution function can be approximated by the cumulative standard normal distribution function as:

$$\Phi\left\langle \frac{\left(\frac{x}{k+\lambda}\right)^h - \left\{1 + hp\left[h-1-\frac{mp(2-h)}{2}\right]\right\}}{h\sqrt{2p}\cdot\left(1+\frac{mp}{2}\right)} \right\rangle$$

(4.2)

where

$$h = 1 - \frac{2}{3}\cdot\frac{(k+\lambda)(k+3\lambda)}{(k+2\lambda)^2}$$

$$p = \frac{k+2\lambda}{(k+\lambda)^2}$$

$$m = (h-1)(1-3h)$$

(4.3)

Setting the confidence level to 1 percent and the degree of freedom to one, the corresponding quantile x can easily be backed out as:

$$x = \left\langle \Phi^{-1}(1\%)\cdot h\sqrt{2p}\cdot\left(1+\frac{mp}{2}\right) + \left\{1+hp\left[h-1-\frac{mp(2-h)}{2}\right]\right\} \right\rangle^{\frac{1}{h}}(1+\lambda)$$

$$\approx \left\langle 2.3264\cdot h\sqrt{2p}\cdot\left(1+\frac{mp}{2}\right) + \left\{1+hp\left[h-1-\frac{mp(2-h)}{2}\right]\right\} \right\rangle^{\frac{1}{h}}(1+\lambda)$$

Thus one-day VaR amount for a currency option can be calculated analytically as:

One-day VaR amount

$$\approx \frac{Gamma}{2}\cdot[S(t)]^2\cdot\left\{SD\left[\frac{dS(t)}{S(t)}\right]\right\}^2$$

$$\cdot\left\langle \frac{2.3264h\sqrt{2p}\cdot\left(1+\frac{mp}{2}\right)}{+\left\{1+hp\left[h-1-\frac{mp(2-h)}{2}\right]\right\}} \right\rangle^{\frac{1}{h}}(1+\lambda) - \frac{Delta^2}{2\cdot Gamma}$$

(4.4)

where

$$\lambda = \left\{ \frac{\dfrac{Delta}{Gamma \cdot S(t)}}{SD\left[\dfrac{dS(t)}{S(t)}\right]} \right\}^2$$

$$h = 1 - \frac{2}{3} \cdot \frac{(1+\lambda)(1+3\lambda)}{(1+2\lambda)^2}$$

$$p = \frac{1+2\lambda}{(1+\lambda)^2}$$

$$m = (h-1)(1-3h) \tag{4.5}$$

This becomes a very convenient closed-form approximation with which to calculate the one-day VaR amount for a currency option. This VaR methodology combining the Delta-Gamma VaR and noncentral Chi-squared distribution is referred to as Delta-Gamma noncentral Chi-squared VaR methodology.

The major drawback of Delta-Gamma noncentral Chi-squared VaR methodology is the overlay of two approximations, one using only the linear and quadratic terms to approximate the change in currency option value and the other one using the cumulative standard normal distribution function to approximate the cumulative noncentral Chi-squared distribution function. The compound effect of these two approximations may introduce larger error to the one-day VaR amount calculation.

4.1.2 *Kupiec-Lopez test*

By definition, an accurate methodology to calculate one-day VaR amounts at the 99th percentile confidence level will register on average 1 percent exceptions over a sufficiently long period of time. An aggressive VaR methodology downwardly biased to produce smaller one-day VaR amounts will result in too many violations, while a conservative VaR methodology upwardly biased to produce larger one-day VaR amounts will result in too few violations.

Kupiec (1995) and Lopez (1996) proposed a relatively powerful two-tailed test for assessing statistically the accuracy of a VaR methodology. For a VaR methodology producing independent one-day VaR amounts with P violations over a period of Q consecutive trading days, the Kupiec-Lopez statistic

$$-2\ln\left[(1-1\%)^{Q-P} \cdot (1\%)^P\right] + 2\ln\left[\left(1-\frac{P}{Q}\right)^{Q-P} \cdot \left(\frac{P}{Q}\right)^P\right] \tag{4.6}$$

forms a Chi-squared distribution with one degree of freedom.

Therefore, the Delta-Gamma VaR noncentral Chi-squared VaR methodology can be tested empirically with the Kupiec-Lopez test over a sufficiently long period of trading days, subject to the availability of historical data.

4.2 Analysis approach

A back testing similar to that proposed by the BCBS (2006) is adopted to assess the performance of the Delta-Gamma noncentral Chi-squared VaR methodology proposed in section 4.1, using the volatility calculated by the quadratic approximation studied in Chapter 3.

For a particular currency option combination specified by the underlying currency, standard maturity, moneyness and option type, a back testing is performed with the following steps:

- On a trading day, the volatility of a currency option is calculated with quadratic approximation;
- This volatility is engaged in calculating the Delta and Gamma of the currency option;
- A one-day VaR amount is computed using the Delta-Gamma noncentral Chi-squared VaR methodology;
- The value of the currency option is calculated again with the updated market data on the next trading day;
- The difference between the currency option values for the two trading days contributes to the loss of the currency option;
- If the loss of the currency option exceeds the one-day VaR amount calculated on the previous trading day, a violation is registered;
- This daily back testing is repeated over a sufficiently long period of consecutive trading days and results in a few violations for a currency option group specified by underlying currency, standard maturity, moneyness and option type. If, after comparison with the critical value suggested by the Kupiec-Lopez test, the number of violations is too small or too large, then the Delta-Gamma noncentral Chi-squared VaR mythology is considered to be less accurate when it is applied to that particular currency option combination.

The SMA is adopted to estimate the standard deviation of the drifts over a historical period of 250 trading days to avoid the use of the *ad hoc* daily decay factor in EWMA that was calibrated by the J.P. Morgan 20 years ago.

4.2.1 Scenarios

The back testing is conducted under three market conditions:

- Major currencies: the seven currencies with the largest volume of transactions in the international foreign exchange market (BIS, 2012), during the period from 2010 to 2012. This market condition represents the typical situation under which the assumptions of the Vanna-Volga method and the Delta-Gamma noncentral Chi-squared VaR methodology are applicable;

- Stress: the seven currencies with the largest volume of transactions in the international foreign exchange market during the period from July 2008 to June 2009, when the financial tsunami of 2008 hit. This market condition represents situations that deviate from the underlying assumptions of the theory of the Vanna-Volga method and the Delta-Gamma noncentral Chi-squared VaR methodology; and
- CNY: the CNY during the period from 2010 to 2012. The CNY is a currency under a government's foreign exchange control and also deviates from the underlying assumptions of the theory of the Vanna-Volga method and the Delta-Gamma noncentral Chi-squared VaR methodology.

4.2.2 Unit of analysis

The unit of analysis is a currency option specified by its underlying currency, standard maturity, moneyness, option type and transaction date. A currency option group is formed by a number of currency options with the same underlying currency, standard maturity, moneyness and option type over a sufficiently long period of consecutive trading days.

4.2.3 Variables

A currency option group is specified by four identification variables. Each currency option in the currency option group is further identified by a transaction day. The one-day VaR amount and the daily loss as intermediate variables are calculated by the independent variables. The violation is determined by comparing the one-day VaR amount and the daily loss.

(a) Identification variables

Each currency option is specified by four identification variables:

- Underlying currency: same as the underlying currency specified in section 3.2.6;
- Standard maturity: same as the standard maturity specified in section 3.2.6;
- Moneyness: same as the tenor specified in section 3.2.6;
- Option type: the currency option is either a Call Option or a Put Option;
- Transaction date: same as the transaction date specified in section 3.2.6.

(b) Independent variables

A one-day VaR amount is calculated with the following five independent variables:

- Market rate of underlying currency: same as the market rate of underlying currency specified in section 3.2.6;

- Strike rate: same as the strike rate of underlying currency specified in section 3.2.6;
- Volatility: the volatility is calculated by using the quadratic approximation of the Vanna-Volga method studied in Chapter 3;
- Domestic risk-free rate: same as the domestic risk-free rate specified in section 3.2.6;
- Foreign risk-free rate: same as the foreign risk free rate specified in section 3.2.6; and
- Maturity: same as the maturity specified in section 3.2.6.

(c) Intermediate variable

There are two intermediate variables:

- One-day VaR amount: the one-day VaR amount is calculated by the Delta-Gamma noncentral Chi-squared VaR methodology proposed in section 4.1.
- Daily loss: the daily loss is the difference between the value of a currency option on the current trading day and the value of the same currency option on the previous trading day.

(d) Dependent variable

- Violation: the one-day VaR amount calculated on the previous trading day is compared with the daily loss observed on the next trading day. If the daily loss on current trading day exceeds the one-day VaR amount calculated on previous trading day, a violation is registered.

4.2.4 Measurement

The accuracy of a VaR methodology is measured by the number of violations. If the actual loss on current trading day exceeds the one-day VaR amount calculated at the end of previous trading day, a violation is registered. In a statistical sense, a VaR methodology is considered to be accurate if over a sufficient long period of consecutive trading days the percentage of trading days on which violations are registered approaches 1 percent.

4.2.5 Sample selection

The specification of the samples selected for back testing is set out in Table 4.1. The major currency analysis comprises seven major currencies, six standard maturities, six moneynesses, two option types and 750 trading days, a total of 378,000 samples. The stress analysis comprises seven major currencies, six standard maturities, six moneynesses, two option types and 250 trading days, a total of 126,000 samples. The CNY analysis comprises the CNY, six times to maturity, six moneynesses, two options and 750 trading days, a total of 54,000 samples.

Table 4.1 Sample selection of VaR back testing

(A) Major currency analysis

Currency	EUR, GBP, CHF, SEK, CAD, JPY, AUD		
Standard maturity	1, 2, 3, 6, 9 and 12 months		
Moneyness	Left and right 35-Delta	Left and right 15-Delta	Left and right 10-Delta
Option type	Call Option and Put Option		
Date	750 trading days during the period from 2010 to 2012		
No. of samples	378,000		

(B) Stress analysis

Currency	EUR, GBP, CHF, SEK, CAD, JPY, AUD		
Maturity	1, 2, 3, 6, 9 and 12 months		
Moneyness	Left and right 35-Delta	Left and right 15-Delta	Left and right 10-Delta
Option type	Call Option and Put Option		
Date	250 trading days during the period July 2008 to June 2009		
No. of samples	126,000		

(C) CNY analysis

Currency	CNY		
Maturity	1, 2, 3, 6, 9 and 12 months		
Moneyness	Left and right 35-Delta	Left and right 15-Delta	Left and right 10-Delta
Date	750 trading days during the period from 2010 to 2012		
No. of samples	54,000		

4.2.6 Secondary data collection

This is the same as the secondary data collection specified in section 3.2.8.

4.2.7 Data analysis

The data analysis is divided into two stages. At the first stage, for each scenario, a Kupiec-Lopez test is conducted to assess the accuracy of the Delta-Gamma non-central Chi-squared VaR methodology on per currency option group basis. The currency option groups rejected by the Kupiec-Lopez are then selected for further investigation.

During the second stage, for each scenario the rejected currency options are examined to identify whether there are any systematic biases. The reasons for the systematic biases are identified.

4.2.8 Hypothesis construction

To test the accuracy of the Delta-Gamma noncentral Chi-squared VaR methodology with regard to a particular currency option group, a Chi-squared test at the 95th percentile confidence level is proposed:

$H2_0$: Percentage of violations $= 1\%$

$H2_a$: Percentage of violations $\neq 1\%$

The hypothesis is tested with the Kupiec-Lopez statistic

$$-2\ln\left[\left(1-1\%\right)^{Q-P}\cdot\left(1\%\right)^{P}\right]+2\ln\left[\left(1-\frac{P}{Q}\right)^{Q-P}\cdot\left(\frac{P}{Q}\right)^{P}\right]$$

where P is number of violations and Q is number of samples.

The critical value is 3.8415 at the 95th percentile confidence level. In other words, at the 95th percentile confidence level, a VaR methodology producing one-day VaR amounts should be rejected if the number of violations is:

- Fewer than 4 or more than 13 for a period of 750 consecutive trading days; and
- Fewer than 1 or more than 5 for a period of 250 consecutive trading days.

4.3 Results and discussions

4.3.1 Major currency test

Table 4.2 lists the number of violations for each currency option combination under the major currency test. A total of 416 out of 504 (82.54 percent) currency option groups pass the Kupiec-Lopez test, with the number of violations falling between 4 and 13 over a period of 750 consecutive trading days.

A total of 25 currency options combinations are rejected by the Kupiec-Lopez test with the number of violations falling above 13, and a total of 61 currency options series are rejected by the Kupiec-Lopez test with the number of exceptions below 4.

The violations essentially demonstrate two systemic observations:

- Too many violations have been produced for 26 currency options groups (18 OTM Call Option combinations and 8 OTM Put Option groups) with short maturities; and
- Too few violations have been produced for 61 currency options combinations with GBP as the underlying currency.

Table 4.2 Number of violations under the major currency test

Ccy	Std. maturity	Option	Moneyness					
			−0.1	−0.15	−0.35	0.35	0.15	0.1
EUR	1	Call	12	12	12	15	26	34
		Put	13	13	12	9	8	8
	2	Call	12	12	12	12	16	19
		Put	13	13	11	9	9	9
	3	Call	12	12	12	12	13	15
		Put	11	11	10	9	9	9
	6	Call	12	12	12	12	12	13
		Put	11	11	10	9	9	9
	9	Call	12	12	12	12	12	12
		Put	10	10	9	9	9	10
	12	Call	12	12	12	12	12	12
		Put	10	10	9	9	9	9
GBP	1	Call	2	2	2	3	11	20
		Put	5	4	4	2	2	2
	2	Call	2	2	2	3	4	4
		Put	4	4	3	2	2	2
	3	Call	2	2	2	3	3	3
		Put	4	4	2	2	2	2
	6	Call	2	2	2	3	3	3
		Put	3	2	2	2	2	2
	9	Call	2	2	3	3	3	2
		Put	2	2	2	2	2	2
	12	Call	2	2	2	3	3	3
		Put	2	2	2	2	2	2
CHF	1	Call	5	5	5	5	12	15
		Put	21	18	12	10	10	10
	2	Call	5	5	5	5	5	7
		Put	14	13	12	10	10	10
	3	Call	5	5	5	5	5	5
		Put	12	12	11	10	10	10
	6	Call	5	5	5	5	5	5
		Put	12	11	11	10	10	10
	9	Call	5	5	5	5	5	5
		Put	11	10	10	10	10	11
	12	Call	5	5	5	5	5	5
		Put	11	11	10	10	10	10
SEK	1	Call	10	10	12	13	19	22
		Put	25	14	6	5	5	5
	2	Call	12	12	12	12	13	13
		Put	9	9	5	5	5	5
	3	Call	12	12	12	12	12	12
		Put	5	5	5	5	5	5
	6	Call	12	12	12	12	12	12
		Put	5	5	5	5	5	5

Table 4.2 (Continued)

Ccy	Std. maturity	Option	Moneyness					
			−0.1	−0.15	−0.35	0.35	0.15	0.1
	9	Call	12	12	12	12	12	12
		Put	5	5	5	5	5	5
	12	Call	12	12	12	12	12	12
		Put	5	5	5	5	5	5
JPY	1	Call	11	11	11	12	15	16
		Put	12	9	8	6	6	6
	2	Call	11	11	11	12	12	12
		Put	8	8	7	6	6	6
	3	Call	12	11	12	12	12	12
		Put	7	7	7	6	6	6
	6	Call	12	12	12	12	12	12
		Put	7	7	7	7	7	7
	9	Call	12	12	12	12	12	12
		Put	7	7	7	7	7	7
	12	Call	12	12	12	12	12	12
		Put	7	7	7	7	7	7
CAD	1	Call	11	11	11	12	19	21
		Put	26	17	4	4	4	4
	2	Call	12	12	12	12	12	14
		Put	11	7	4	4	4	4
	3	Call	12	12	12	12	12	12
		Put	5	4	4	4	4	4
	6	Call	12	12	12	12	12	12
		Put	4	4	4	4	4	4
	9	Call	12	12	12	12	12	12
		Put	4	4	4	4	4	4
	12	Call	12	12	12	12	12	12
		Put	4	4	4	4	4	4
AUD	1	Call	10	10	10	11	24	40
		Put	13	12	8	8	8	8
	2	Call	10	10	10	10	14	18
		Put	9	8	8	8	8	8
	3	Call	10	10	10	10	11	13
		Put	8	8	8	8	8	8
	6	Call	10	10	10	10	10	10
		Put	8	8	8	8	8	8
	9	Call	10	10	10	10	10	10
		Put	8	8	8	8	8	8
	12	Call	10	10	10	10	10	10
		Put	8	8	8	8	8	8

OTM currency options with short maturities are currency options that will expire in a short period of time, and the market rates of the underlying currency are far from their corresponding strike rates. These currency options will have a very low chance of resulting in a positive payoff at maturity. Therefore, the value of an OTM currency option with a short maturity is very low, usually approaching zero. Moreover, these currency options are thinly traded in the market. Thus, the theoretical value is very sensitive to the deviation of the underlying theories. Moreover, it has been demonstrated in Chapter 3 that the accuracy of quadratic approximation starts to deteriorate when it is utilized to extrapolate volatilities. Therefore, it is not surprising to observe that excessive violations are found with OTM currency options with short maturities. The same issue is not observed for ITM currency options, whose value is dominated by the difference between the market value of the underlying currency and the strike rate. As such, the accuracy of the volatility has a small impact on the ITM currency options when the Delta-Gamma noncentral Chi-squared methodology is utilized to calculate the one-day VaR amounts.

For currency options with GBP as the underlying currency, the one-day VaR amounts are too large to represent the market risk of the currency options across most standard maturities, moneynesses and option types. The overall result suggests that the SMA is an upwardly biased estimator for predicting the standard deviation of GBP.

The quality of the SMA standard deviation estimator is further assessed by the normalized daily drift, which is the daily drift divided by the standard deviation estimated by the SMA on the previous trading day. If the SMA is accurate in estimating the standard deviation, over a long period of trading days the normalized daily drifts should form a set of standard normal random numbers. Define the normalized mean, normalized standard deviation, normalized skewness and normalized kurtosis as the mean, standard deviation, skewness and kurtosis of the normalized daily return. A normalized standard deviation below one suggests that the standard deviation estimated by the SMA may be too large, while a normalized standard deviation above one suggests that the standard deviation estimated by the SMA may be too small.

The mean, standard deviation, skewness and kurtosis of the normalized daily drift for the seven major currencies over the testing period of 750 trading days are listed in Table 4.3. Among the seven major currencies, the normalized daily drift of the GBP has the smallest normalized mean (0.0038), normalized standard deviation (0.8943), normalized skewness (−0.0997) and normalized kurtosis (2.9077). Thus, the standard deviation estimated by the SMA becomes too large to characterize the dispersion of the daily drift of the GBP. For other major currencies, although the normalized standard deviations are also below one, the effect from the overestimated standard deviation is offset by the effect from the fat tail kurtosis over three.

In practice, the overestimation of the standard deviation drives financial institution to be more conservative in managing their currency options. This may affect the profits of financial institutions. The situation can be mitigated by estimating the standard deviation of the daily drift of the GBP with the EWMA. The original decay factor of 0.94 is adopted in the EMWA standard deviation estimator.

The results are shown in Table 4.4. A total of 70 out of 72 currency option series pass the Kupiec-Lopez test, with the number of violations falling between 4 and 13 over a period of 750 consecutive trading days. Two OTM Call Option groups

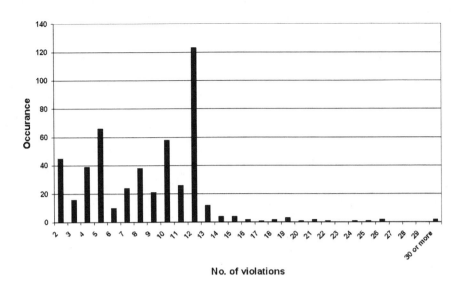

Figure 4.1 Summary of number of violations

Table 4.3 Distribution parameters of the normalized daily drifts under the major currency test

Currency	Mean	S.D.	Skewness	Kurtosis
EUR	−0.0155	0.9718	−0.1468	3.6295
GBP	0.0038	0.8943	−0.0997	2.9077
CHF	0.0409	0.9963	−0.7178	13.2629
SEK	0.0162	0.9264	−0.2572	3.5695
JPY	0.0076	0.9180	−0.3552	6.9198
CAD	0.0041	0.8977	−0.3234	4.1995
AUD	0.0144	0.9258	−0.1819	4.8980

Table 4.4 No. of violations for GBP with the EWMA

Ccy	Std. maturity	Option	Moneyness					
			−0.1	−0.15	−0.35	0.35	0.15	0.1
GBP	1	Call	6	6	6	7	16	28
		Put	12	11	4	4	4	4
	2	Call	6	6	6	6	7	8
		Put	5	4	4	4	4	4
	3	Call	6	6	6	6	7	7
		Put	4	4	4	4	4	4
	6	Call	6	6	6	6	6	6
		Put	4	4	4	4	4	4
	9	Call	6	6	6	6	6	6
		Put	4	4	4	4	4	4
	12	Call	6	6	6	6	6	6
		Put	4	4	4	4	4	4

with short maturities are rejected by the Kupiec-Lopez test, suggesting that the one-day VaR amounts are too low in representing the market risk of those two OTM Call Option groups. The results are in line with the currency options with other underlying currencies.

4.3.2 Stress analysis

Table 4.5 lists the number of violations for each currency option group under the stress test. All 504 currency option groups failed the Kupiec-Lopez test, with seven or more violations over a stress period of 250 consecutive trading days.

The stress test suggests that the Delta-Gamma VaR noncentral Chi-squared VaR methodology understates the one-day VaR amounts under stress conditions. This observation is explained by the distribution parameters of the normalized daily drift exhibited in Table 4.6. The normalized standard deviations are well

Table 4.5 Number of violations under the stress test

Ccy	Std. maturity	Option	Moneyness					
			−0.1	−0.15	−0.35	0.35	0.15	0.1
EUR	**1,2,3**	**Call**	9 to 12					
	6,9,12	**Put**	13 to 14					
GBP	**1,2,3**	**Call**	19 to 24					
	6,9,12	**Put**	7 to 8					
CHF	**1,2,3**	**Call**	7 to 10					
	6,9,12	**Put**	7 to 9					
SEK	**1,2,3**	**Call**	14 to 15					
	6,9,12	**Put**	14 to 20					
JPY	**1,2,3**	**Call**	6 to 13					
	6,9,12	**Put**	10 to 12					
CAD	**1,2,3**	**Call**	12 to 19					
	6,9,12	**Put**	8 to 14					
AUD	**1,2,3**	**Call**	9 to 19					
	6,9,12	**Put**	7 to 12					

Table 4.6 Distribution parameters of the normalized daily drifts under the stress test

Currency	Mean	S.D.	Skewness	Kurtosis
EUR	−0.0677	1.2852	−0.0543	4.2819
GBP	0.0886	1.3358	−0.0905	4.4102
CHF	−0.0459	1.1275	0.1049	5.6834
SEK	−0.1633	1.4389	0.0855	4.1235
JPY	−0.0561	1.3169	0.0213	4.7572
CAD	−0.0404	1.1135	0.0066	5.7692
AUD	−0.0826	1.2632	−0.0599	6.1771

above one, suggesting that the standard deviations estimated by the SMA are too small to characterize the dispersion of the daily drift. Moreover, the normalized kurtosises are consistently above three, illustrating the fact that the daily drift of currency rate does not follow the normality assumption underlying the Delta-Gamma noncentral Chi-squared VaR methodology. The combined effect of the normalized standard deviation and the normalized kurtosis thus increases the number of violations.

4.3.3 CNY analysis

Table 4.7 lists the number of violations for each currency option series under the CNY test. All 72 currency option series fail the Kupiec-Lopez test, with 25 or more violations over a stress period of 750 consecutive trading days.

The CNY test suggests that the Delta-Gamma noncentral Chi-squared VaR methodology understates the one-day VaR amounts for the CNY. This observation is explained by the distribution parameters of the normalized daily drift for the CNY exhibited in Table 4.8. The normalized standard deviation is materially above one, suggesting that the standard deviations estimated by the SMA are too small to characterize the dispersion of the daily drift. Moreover, the normalized kurtosis is materially above three, demonstrating the fact that the daily drift of the CNY does not follow the normality assumption that underlies the Delta-Gamma noncentral Chi-squared VaR methodology.

Table 4.7 Number of violations for the CNY test

Ccy	Std. maturity	Option	Moneyness					
			−0.1	−0.15	−0.35	0.35	0.15	0.1
CNY	1	Call	25	25	25	29	31	38
		Put	48	46	39	34	34	38
	2	Call	25	25	25	27	28	30
		Put	42	40	36	35	34	36
	3	Call	25	25	25	26	27	27
		Put	38	36	35	35	35	36
	6	Call	26	26	26	26	26	26
		Put	35	35	35	35	35	36
	9	Call	26	26	26	26	26	26
		Put	35	35	35	35	35	35
	12	Call	26	26	26	26	26	26
		Put	35	35	35	35	35	35

Table 4.8 Distribution parameters of the normalized daily drifts for the CNY

Currency	Mean	S.D	Skewness	Kurtosis
CNY	0.1245	1.3216	1.0649	10.0232

4.4 Conclusions

A Delta-Gamma noncentral Chi-squared VaR methodology is developed to calculate the one-day VaR amount for currency options in closed-form solution. The quadratic approximation is utilized to estimate the volatility of the currency options.

Back testing is conducted to assess the performance of the Delta-Gamma noncentral Chi-squared VaR methodology for:

- The major currencies under the regular market conditions;
- The major currencies under the stress market conditions; and
- The CNY under the regular market conditions

where the volatility of the currency options are calculated in accordance with the quadratic approximation of the Vanna-Volga method. Kupiec-Lopez test is adopted as the statistical test to determine the accuracy of this VaR methodology.

The back testing reveals that the Delta-Gamma noncentral Chi-squared VaR methodology is:

- In general, an appropriate methodology to calculate the one-day VaR amounts for the major currencies under the regular market conditions; and
- Not an appropriate methodology to calculate the one-day VaR amounts for the major currencies under stress market conditions and CNY.

In contrast to the situations of volatility recovery, the strike rates of the currency options have little systematic impact on the accuracy of the one-day VaR amount calculations.

Under the major currency test, the one-day VaR amounts for OTM currency options may be too low to represent the market risk of currency options due to the combined effort of the low currency option value, low market liquidity and the deteriorated performance of the quadratic approximation. In addition, the one-day VaR amounts for those currency options with GBP as underlying currency appear to be too high to represent the market risk of those currency options. The observation is explained by the fact that the SMA is a downwardly biased standard deviation estimator that results in too large standard deviations for the GBP. The situation can be mitigated with the EWMA as the standard deviation estimator.

5 Dynamic portfolio replication

This chapter examines the relative performance of the Vanna-Volga method in dynamic portfolio replication, which is one of the major daily tasks of currency option traders. Dynamic portfolio replication seeks to replicate a currency option with the underlying currency and domestic cash on the basis of the self-finance replicating strategy with continued rebalancing. This replicated portfolio is then utilized to hedge the currency option, one of the major tasks of currency traders in the currency option market. While the Black-Scholes model hedge only the variation of a currency option arising from the underlying currency, the Vanna-Volga method essentially extends the hedging to the variations of a currency option arising from volatility and the combined effect arising from the currency rate and the volatility, providing more flexibility in terms of hedging.

5.1 Theoretical framework

Under the assumption that the risk-free rates r_d and r_f are constant, for a currency option X, the Vanna-Volga method suggests the following replication strategy:

- At time t, a replicating portfolio $R(t)$ of currency option X is formed with (i) $w_0(t)$ underlying currency; (ii) $w_1(t)$, $w_2(t)$ and $w_3(t)$ liquidly traded options X_1, X_2 and X_3; and (iii) domestic cash amount $z(t)$ put in a money market account, where $w_1(t)$, $w_2(t)$ and $w_3(t)$ are calculated by equation (3.13), that is:

$$V(t) = R(t)$$
$$= w_0(t)S(t) + \sum_{k=1}^{3} w_k(t)V_k(t) + z(t) \tag{5.1}$$

- At time $t + dt$, the replicating portfolio evolves to $R(t + dt)$ and consists of (i) $w_0(t)$ underlying currency; (ii) the interest $w_0(t)S(t)r_f dt$ generated by the underlying currency; (iii) $w_1(t)$, $w_2(t)$ and $w_3(t)$ liquidly traded options X_1,

X_2 and X_3; and (iv) domestic cash amount $(1 + r_d dt)z(t)$ in a money market account, that is:

$$R(t + dt) = w_0(t)S(t + dt) + w_0(t)S(t + dt)r_f dt$$
$$+ \sum_{k=1}^{3} w_3(t)V_3(t + dt) + (1 + r_d dt)z(t) \tag{5.2}$$

The replicating portfolio is rebalanced with $w_1(t + dt)$, $w_2(t + dt)$ and $w_3(t + dt)$ calculated according to equation (3.12). The domestic cash surplus or deflect as a result of rebalancing is deposited to or withdrawn from the money account to arrive at a new cash amount $z(t + dt)$. The value of the replicating portfolio is now the same as the value of the currency option $V(t + dt)$, that is:

$$V(t + dt) = R(t + dt)$$
$$= w_0(t + dt)S(t + dt) + \sum_{k=1}^{3} w_1(t + dt)V_1(t + dt) + z(t + dt) \tag{5.3}$$

- The rebalancing process is repeated continuously until maturity T. Then the terminal payoff of currency option X should be equal to the weighted sum of (i) the value of the underlying currency; (ii) the payoffs of the three liquidly traded currency options; and (iii) the amount of domestic cash in the money market account, that is:

$$Payoff[X] = R(T)$$
$$= w_0(T)S(T) + \sum_{k=1}^{3} w_k(T)V(T) + z(T)$$
$$= w_0(T)S(T) + \sum_{k=1}^{3} w_k(T)Payoff[X_k] + z(T) \tag{5.4}$$

In practice, the rebalancing could be performed only on a discrete time basis, for example once a day. Moreover, the slightly shift of the risk-free rates may also impact the replication performance, although immaterially.

A more material replication error is introduced because of the regime switching during the rebalancing process. While the hedging ratios are calculated with a single Black-Scholes volatility, the actual replication is essentially conducted with the market prices of the three liquidly traded options.

From equation (5.1), using the self-financing argument:

$$V^{BS}(t) = w_0(t)S(t) + \sum_{k=1}^{3} w_k(t)V_k^{BS}(t) + z(t)$$

$$dV(t) = w_0(t)dS(t) + w_0(t)S(t)\cdot r_f dt$$

$$+ \sum_{k=1}^{3} w_k(t)dV_k(t) + z(t)\cdot r_d dt$$

$$= w_0(t)dS(t) + w_0(t)S(t)\cdot qdt + \sum_{k=1}^{3} w_k(t)dV_k(t)$$

$$+ \left[V^{BS}(t) - w_0(t)S(t) + \sum_{k=1}^{3} w_k(t)V_k^{BS}(t) \right]\cdot r_d dt \qquad (5.5)$$

Define the replication error as:

$$\varepsilon(t) = V^{VV}(t) - R(t)$$

$$d\varepsilon(t) = dV^{VV}(t) - dR(t)$$

$$= d\left\{ V^{BS}(t) + \sum_{k=1}^{3} w_k(t)\left[V_k^{Market}(t) - V_k^{BS}(t) \right] \right\}$$

$$- d\left[w_0(t)S(t) + \sum_{k=1}^{3} w_k(t)V_k^{Mkt}(t) + z(t) \right]$$

$$= \left\{ \begin{array}{l} \left[dV^{BS}(t) + \sum_{k=1}^{3} w_k(t)\left[dV_k^{Market}(t) - dV_k^{BS}(t) \right] \right] \\[2mm] + \sum_{k=1}^{3} \left[V_k^{Market}(t) - V_k^{BS}(t) \right] dw_k(t) \end{array} \right.$$

$$- \left\{ \begin{array}{l} \left[w_0(t)dS(t) + w_0(t)S(t)\cdot r_f dt \right. \\[2mm] + \sum_{k=1}^{3} w_k(t)dV_k^{Mkt}(t) + z(t)\cdot r_d dt \end{array} \right.$$

$$= w_0(t)dS(t) + w_0(t)S(t) \cdot r_f dt + \sum_{k=1}^{3} w_k(t)dV_k(t)$$

$$+ \left[V^{BS}(t) - w_0(t)S(t) + \sum_{k=1}^{3} w_k(t)V_k^{BS}(t) \right] r_d dt$$

$$- \left[w_0(t)dS(t) + w_0(t)S(t) \cdot qdt + \sum_{k=1}^{3} w_k(t)dV_k(t) \right]$$

$$- \left[R(t) - w_0(t)S(t) - \sum_{k=1}^{3} w_k(t)V_k^{Market}(t) \right] r_d dt$$

$$+ \sum_{k=1}^{3} \left[V_k^{Market}(t) - V_k^{BS}(t) \right] dw_k(t)$$

$$= \left\{ V^{BS}(t) + \sum_{k=1}^{3} w_k(t) \left[V_k^{Market}(t) - V_k^{BS}(t) \right] - R(t) \right\} r_d dt$$

$$+ \sum_{k=1}^{3} \left[V_k^{Market}(t) - V_k^{BS}(t) \right] dw_k(t)$$

$$= \left[V^{VV}(t) - R(t) \right] r_d dt + \sum_{k=1}^{3} \left[V_k^{Market}(t) - V_k^{BS}(t) \right] dw_k(t)$$

$$= \varepsilon(t) \cdot r_d dt + \sum_{k=1}^{3} \left[V_k^{Market}(t) - V_k^{BS}(t) \right] dw_k(t) \tag{5.6}$$

Solving this differential equation, the replication error is obtained as:

$$\varepsilon(T) = \int_0^T \left\{ \exp\left[r_d(T-t) \right] \sum_{k=1}^{3} \left[V_k^{Market}(t) - V_k^{BS}(t) \right] dw_k(t) \right\} \tag{5.7}$$

Equation (5.7) provides an insight to the replication accuracy of Vanna-Volga method:

- The longer the maturity, the larger the total replication error; and
- The greater the difference between the market prices and the Black-Scholes values of the three liquid options, the larger the total replication error.

The insight also suggests that although the ATM volatility may not be an optimal choice for Black-Scholes volatility, it serves as a good choice since the use of the ATM volatility as the Black-Scholes volatility eliminates one term in the summation, thereby effectively reducing the replication error.

Although theoretically intuitive, this replication strategy involves the computation of prices, higher-order Greeks and hedging ratios of the three liquidly traded currency options.

A further simplification can be performed with the quadratic approximation of the implied volatility studied in Chapter 3. Through quadratic approximation, the information about the three liquidly traded currency options is consolidated into one single volatility. Indeed, in accordance with the Black-Scholes model, the three liquidly traded options X_1, X_2 and X_3 can also be replicated with the underlying currency and domestic cash, subject to three individual hedge ratios calculated by the corresponding volatilities. This argument thus provides a simple alternative to the dynamic portfolio replication of a currency option under the Vanna-Volga method: a currency option can simply be replicated with underlying currency and domestic cash with a single hedge ratio calculated by the volatility derived from the three liquidly traded currency options. Where the quadratic approximation has demonstrated an adequate degree of accuracy in calculating the volatility at an arbitrary strike rate K with a simple set up, this volatility can also be used to calculate the hedging ratios.

5.2 Analysis approach

The relative performance of dynamic portfolio replication with the time-varied implied volatility, domestic interest rate and foreign interest rate incorporated is assessed in this section.

At the origination, a currency option with standard maturity and moneyness is replicated with the underlying currency and domestic cash, where the hedge ratio is calculated by the volatility observed directly from the market at origination. This replicating portfolio is rebalanced in accordance with a self-finance trading strategy on every standard rebalancing day with the updated volatility derived from the quadratic approximation, domestic interest rate and foreign interest rate. At maturity, the difference between the values of the replicating portfolio and the payoff of the currency option represents the replication error arising from the Vanna-Volga method, referred to as the VV replication error.

The same currency option is also replicated in accordance with the Black-Scholes framework under which the volatility, domestic interest rate and foreign interest rate remain constant throughout the life the currency option. Another replication error, referred to as the BS replication error, is derived as the difference between the values of the replicating portfolio and the payoff of the currency option. This forms the replication error arising from the Black-Scholes framework, referred to as the BS replication error.

The VV and BS replication errors are then compared. A smaller replication error represents a superior approach for the application of dynamic portfolio replication.

5.2.1 Scenarios

The dynamic portfolio replication is conducted under three market conditions:

- Major currencies: the seven currencies with the largest volume of transactions in the international foreign exchange market (BIS, 2012), during the period from 2010 to 2012. This market condition represents the typical situation under which the assumptions of the Vanna-Volga method are applicable;
- Stress: the seven currencies with the largest volume of transactions in the international foreign exchange market, during the period from 2008 to 2009, when the financial tsunami of 2008 hit. This market condition represents the situation that deviates from the underlying assumptions on the theory of the Vanna-Volga method; and
- CNY: the CNY during the period from 2010 to 2012. The CNY is a currency under government's foreign exchange control and also deviates from the underlying assumptions on the theory of the Vanna-Volga method.

5.2.2 Unit of analysis

The unit of analysis is a currency option specified by its underlying currency, standard maturity, moneyness, option type and transaction date.

5.2.3 Variables

A currency option is specified by five identification variables. Each currency option is rebalanced on the standard rebalancing days where the volatility surface and term structure of interest rates are readily available. The difference between the values of the replicating portfolio and the currency option payoff at maturity forms the replication error that contributes to the dependent variable.

(a) Identification variables

Each currency option is specified by five identification variables:

- Underlying currency: same as the underlying currency specified in section 3.2.6;
- Standard maturity: same as the standard tenor specified in section 3.2.6;
- Moneyness: same as the moneyness specified in section 3.2.6;
- Option type: the currency option is either a Call Option or Put Option;
- Transaction date: same as the transaction date specified in section 3.2.6.

(a) Independent variables

The value of a replicating portfolio is calculated with the following five independent variables:

- Market rate of underlying currency: same as the market rate of underlying currency specified in section 3.2.6;

- Strike rate: same as the strike rate of underlying currency specified in section 3.2.6;
- Volatility: the volatility is observed directly in the market at origination or calculated by using the quadratic approximation of the Vanna-Volga method studied in Chapter 3;
- Domestic risk-free rate: same as the domestic risk-free rate specified in section 3.2.6;
- Foreign risk-free rate: same as the foreign risk free rate specified in section 3.2.6; and
- Maturity: same as the time to maturity specified in section 3.2.6.

(b) Intermediate variable

There are three intermediate variables:

- Rebalancing day: the date on which the rebalancing of a replicating portfolio is performed. The rebalancing essentially occurs at the standard maturities on which the updated volatility of three liquid currency options, domestic interest rates and foreign interest rates are observable;
- Value of replicating portfolio: the value of the replicating portfolio is calculated as the sum of the total market values of the underlying currency and domestic cash in the replicating portfolio;
- Currency option payoff: for a Call Option, the payoff is calculated as (i) the difference between the market rate of underlying currency and the strike rate or (ii) zero, whichever is larger. For a Put Option, the payoff is calculated as (i) the difference between the strike rate and the market rate of underlying currency or (ii) zero, whichever is larger.

(c) Dependent variable

- Replication error: the difference between the value of the replication portfolio and currency option payoff, both at maturity.

5.2.4 Measurement

The accuracy of the dynamic portfolio replication is measured by the replication error, which is the difference between the value of the replicating portfolio and the currency option payoff, both at maturity.

5.2.5 Sample selection

The specification of the samples selected for dynamic portfolio replication is set out in Table 5.1. The major currency analysis comprises seven major currencies, five standard maturities, six moneynesses, two option types and 504 trading days, a total of 211,680 samples. The stress analysis comprises seven major currencies, five standard tenors, six moneynesses, two option types and 254 trading days, a total of 106,680 samples. The CNY analysis comprises the CNY, six standard

Table 5.1 Sample selection for dynamic portfolio replication

(A) Major currency analysis

Currency	EUR, GBP, CHF, SEK, CAD, JPY, AUD		
Standard maturity	2, 3, 6, 9 and 12 months		
Moneyness	Left and right 35-Delta	Left and right 15-Delta	Left and right 10-Delta
Option type	Call Option and Put Option		
Origination date	504 trading days during the period from 2010 to 2011		
No. of samples	216,680		

(B) Stress analysis

Currency	EUR, GBP, CHF, SEK, CAD, JPY, AUD		
Standard maturity	2, 3, 6, 9 and 12 months		
Moneyness	Left and right 35-Delta	Left and right 15-Delta	Left and right 10-Delta
Option type	Call Option and Put Option		
Origination date	254 trading days during the year 2008		
No. of samples	106,680		

(C) CNY analysis

Currency	CNY		
Standard maturity	2, 3, 6, 9 and 12 months		
Moneyness	Left and right 35-Delta	Left and right 15-Delta	Left and right 10-Delta
Origination date	504 trading days during the period from 2010 to 2011		
No. of samples	30,240		

tenors, six moneynesses, two options and 504 trading days, a total of 30,240 samples.

5.2.6 Secondary data collection

This is the same as the secondary data collection specified in section 3.2.8.

5.2.7 Data analysis

The data analysis seeks to compare the VV and BS replication errors in accordance with the average absolute errors. For each combination of currency, standard maturity, moneyness and option type, the averages and t-statistics of VV and BS replication errors are calculated. The t-statistic is compared with a critical value to assess whether statistically the average VV replication error is smaller than the average BS replication error. If the t-statistic is above the critical value, the Vanna-Volga method is statistically inferior to the Black-Scholes framework in terms of dynamic portfolio replication and the reason is investigated.

5.2.8 Hypothesis construction

For each currency option combination, the averages of the VV replication errors and the BS replication errors are tested with a sample mean t-test at the 95th percentile confidence level. This is performed with the following hypothesis:

$H3_0$: Average of VV replication errors < Average of BS replication errors

$H3_a$: Average of VV replication errors > Average of BS replication errors

A t-statistic is constructed such that:

$$t = \frac{Average\ of\ VV\ replication\ errors - Average\ of\ BS\ replication\ errors}{\sqrt{\frac{S.D.\ of\ VV\ replication\ errors^2 + S.D.\ of\ BS\ replication\ errors^2}{No.\ of\ samples}}}$$

with modified degree of freedom

$$df = \frac{No.\ of\ samples \times \left(\begin{array}{c} S.D.\ of\ VV\ replication\ errors^2 + \\ S.D.\ of\ BS\ replication\ errors^2 \end{array}\right)^2}{S.D.\ of\ VV\ replication\ errors^4 + S.D.\ of\ BS\ replication\ errors^4}$$

5.3 Results and discussions

5.3.1 Major currency test

Table 5.2 lists the t-statistics for all currency option groups under the major currency test. For all 420 currency option groups, the t-statistics are well below the critical value 1.96 and the t tests fail to reject the null hypothesis that the average of VV replication errors is smaller than or equal to the average of the BS replication errors. In addition, 290 out of 420 currency option combinations (69.05 percent) registered a negative t-statistic. The results suggest that the Vanna-Volga method generally outperforms the Black-Scholes framework in terms of dynamic portfolio replication, although the confidence level is not sufficiently high.

The negative t-statistics are distributed evenly and randomly among the currency, standard maturity, moneyness and option type and exhibit no systematic trend.

5.3.2 Stress analysis

Table 5.3 lists the t-statistics for all currency option groups under the stress test. The t-statistics of 21 out of 420 (5 percent) currency option groups are larger than the critical value 1.96, thus rejecting the null hypothesis that the average of VV

Table 5.2 t-statistics for major currency test

Ccy	Std. maturity	Option	Moneyness					
			−0.1	*−0.15*	*−0.35*	*0.35*	*0.15*	*0.1*
EUR	2	**Call**	−0.0495	0.2050	0.0690	−0.1151	−0.0281	−0.2988
		Put	−0.0248	−0.0665	−0.0156	0.0264	0.0337	0.0387
	3	**Call**	−0.3513	0.2860	−0.0588	−0.1703	−0.1827	−0.5337
		Put	−0.0678	−0.1337	−0.0968	0.0900	0.0729	0.0450
	6	**Call**	−1.0590	0.1504	−0.6076	−0.6246	−0.9186	−0.2864
		Put	−0.0444	−0.1222	−0.1392	0.0809	0.0150	0.0301
	9	**Call**	−3.4778	−1.3712	−0.8319	0.2629	−0.8747	−0.8191
		Put	−0.0032	−0.0535	−0.0252	0.2609	0.0521	0.0326
	12	**Call**	−7.0520	−2.2196	−0.7820	0.0819	−0.6846	−0.5732
		Put	0.0243	−0.1225	−0.0409	0.1588	−0.0071	−0.0467
GBP	2	**Call**	0.7236	0.6478	−0.1989	−0.2889	−0.0077	0.0356
		Put	−0.0559	−0.0733	0.0213	−0.0667	0.0078	0.0271
	3	**Call**	−0.1257	0.5363	−0.4097	−0.6498	−0.3866	−0.0520
		Put	−0.0721	−0.1646	−0.0469	0.0888	−0.0010	0.0489
	6	**Call**	−5.2912	−1.9150	−0.5184	−1.7240	−0.6828	−0.4943
		Put	−0.0199	−0.1601	−0.1773	−0.1311	0.2560	0.2848
	9	**Call**	−12.9743	−6.7134	−2.7875	−1.6887	−0.7078	−0.3920
		Put	−0.0233	−0.1476	−0.2367	0.2708	0.5374	0.5565
	12	**Call**	−25.0544	−13.2942	−4.7358	−2.1631	−0.6228	−0.1397
		Put	−0.0414	−0.1752	−0.2723	0.4567	0.6824	0.6502
CHF	2	**Call**	−0.3184	−0.4302	−0.3604	−0.2195	0.0388	0.1652
		Put	0.0230	0.0426	0.0819	−0.0418	−0.0680	−0.0755
	3	**Call**	−0.0646	−0.6978	−0.7851	−0.5837	−0.0363	0.2131
		Put	−0.0632	−0.0093	0.0838	0.0484	−0.0798	−0.1476
	6	**Call**	0.5624	0.1098	−1.0876	−0.3776	−0.8531	−0.6887
		Put	−0.0345	−0.0396	−0.2132	−0.1352	−0.0439	−0.1319
	9	**Call**	0.4696	0.2790	−0.8022	−0.5718	−0.4695	−0.3029
		Put	−0.0467	−0.0027	−0.0199	−0.3128	−0.1762	−0.1478
	12	**Call**	−0.0677	0.7329	−0.3252	−1.0914	0.0699	0.1455
		Put	−0.0207	−0.0227	−0.0486	−0.2278	−0.2984	−0.3168
SEK	2	**Call**	−0.1763	−0.0873	−0.1032	−0.2481	−0.3639	−0.7882
		Put	−0.0159	−0.0497	−0.1236	−0.0932	0.0052	0.0014
	3	**Call**	−0.2747	−0.4271	−0.5980	−0.7734	−0.6931	−1.4363
		Put	−0.0427	−0.1128	−0.2025	−0.0905	−0.0012	−0.0281
	6	**Call**	0.0699	0.5347	−0.7063	−0.4469	−1.5531	−2.0159
		Put	0.0787	0.0246	−0.0493	−0.2103	−0.1573	−0.1419
	9	**Call**	−2.0742	−0.7339	−0.2673	0.4077	−0.9899	−1.7034
		Put	0.1158	0.0936	−0.0737	−0.2728	−0.1737	−0.2550
	12	**Call**	−4.0843	−1.9880	−0.0754	0.6851	−0.5631	−1.0655
		Put	0.1265	0.1255	0.0521	−0.6107	−0.3745	−0.4301
JPY	2	**Call**	0.5769	0.5485	0.0743	−0.0443	−0.3115	−0.1025
		Put	−0.0257	−0.0488	−0.0875	0.0580	0.0017	−0.0242

Ccy	Std. maturity	Option	Moneyness					
			−0.1	*−0.15*	*−0.35*	*0.35*	*0.15*	*0.1*
	3	Call	0.6254	0.9109	0.0289	0.3368	−0.3585	−0.3702
		Put	−0.0094	−0.0548	−0.1457	0.1429	−0.0519	−0.0860
	6	Call	−0.2055	0.0863	0.2804	0.0667	−1.5967	−1.9334
		Put	0.0615	0.0398	−0.2728	−0.0019	−0.2684	−0.2440
	9	Call	−0.3511	1.0182	0.0362	0.3541	−1.9708	−3.0670
		Put	0.0936	0.0113	−0.2869	−0.0626	−0.4915	−0.4842
	12	Call	1.5572	2.6148	0.5876	0.9018	−1.1378	−2.4580
		Put	0.0867	0.0117	−0.2596	−0.3715	−0.7375	−0.7664
CAD	1	Call	−0.1856	−0.2391	0.2440	−0.2268	−0.3100	−0.2816
		Put	−0.0198	−0.0738	−0.1338	−0.0742	0.0364	0.0253
	3	Call	−0.4516	−0.5129	0.2416	−0.3398	−0.8464	−1.0822
		Put	0.0020	−0.0482	−0.1867	−0.1418	−0.0098	0.0053
	6	Call	−1.4555	−0.8718	0.3013	−0.6372	−0.6409	−1.1574
		Put	0.0377	−0.0056	−0.0818	−0.3073	−0.1156	−0.1402
	9	Call	−5.6256	−3.9444	−0.3378	−0.8254	−0.5257	−1.2040
		Put	0.0668	0.0585	−0.1658	−0.1777	−0.0693	−0.1911
	12	Call	−13.9873	−10.9231	−2.6619	−0.9570	−0.1450	−1.2937
		Put	−0.1856	−0.2391	0.2440	−0.2268	−0.3100	−0.2816
AUD	2	Call	−0.1875	0.1006	0.1512	−0.0743	−0.5147	−0.7942
		Put	0.0434	−0.0185	−0.0545	0.0219	0.0568	0.0015
	3	Call	0.1244	0.3398	0.0461	−0.3836	−0.9230	−0.8406
		Put	0.0240	−0.0835	−0.0739	−0.1006	0.0867	0.0563
	6	Call	−1.3655	0.5716	0.1605	0.1701	−1.2580	−2.1055
		Put	0.2548	0.1027	0.0040	−0.0323	−0.0864	−0.1780
	9	Call	−1.3080	1.0454	0.4840	−0.9363	−0.4067	−1.1891
		Put	0.3769	0.2487	−0.0306	−0.1254	−0.2449	−0.0970
	12	Call	−0.1875	0.1006	0.1512	−0.0743	−0.5147	−0.7942
		Put	0.0434	−0.0185	−0.0545	0.0219	0.0568	0.0015

Remark: There are 504 samples in each currency option combination. The critical value at the 95 percent confidence level is 1.96.

replication errors is smaller than or equal to the average of the BS replication errors. In addition, the number of currency option combinations that registered a negative t-statistic was reduced to 280 out of 420 (59 percent). The results suggest that the Vanna-Volga method continues to dominate the Black-Scholes framework in terms of dynamic portfolio replication even under the stress condition, although there is a moderate deterioration in the result.

The negative t-statistics continue to be distributed evenly and randomly among the currency, standard maturity, moneyness and option type and exhibit no systematic trend.

Table 5.3 t-statistics for stress test

Ccy	Std. maturity	Option	Moneyness					
			−0.1	−0.15	−0.35	0.35	0.15	0.1
EUR	2	Call	−0.3399	−0.1630	0.2753	0.7318	1.0538	1.2444
		Put	0.0935	0.0266	−0.2260	−0.1932	−0.0637	−0.0441
	3	Call	−0.0321	0.0995	0.5651	0.6814	1.2224	1.5921
		Put	−0.2615	−0.4002	−0.4374	−0.0561	−0.1084	−0.0857
	6	Call	−0.7358	0.0721	1.2438	1.3019	1.4006	1.6390
		Put	−0.3992	−0.4129	−0.6318	−0.5120	−0.3544	−0.3068
	9	Call	−2.0999	−1.0555	1.2179	2.4770	2.5473	2.7588
		Put	−0.1756	−0.1840	−0.9602	−0.8611	−0.7288	−0.6645
	12	Call	−3.8794	−3.7854	−0.5647	1.0866	1.0028	1.7023
		Put	−0.3348	−0.5503	−0.7215	−0.8037	−1.0158	−0.9615
GBP	2	Call	−0.3196	−0.1919	0.2586	0.9980	1.6258	1.9280
		Put	0.1448	0.0435	−0.1848	−0.1876	−0.1264	−0.0940
	3	Call	0.3767	0.7762	1.2054	1.5726	2.0372	2.4011
		Put	−0.2850	−0.5027	−0.4118	−0.2135	−0.1364	−0.1098
	6	Call	0.9351	1.3445	1.5665	0.4666	0.5027	0.2870
		Put	−0.4519	−0.7138	−0.7062	−0.1839	−0.1775	−0.1649
	9	Call	0.4448	1.0240	2.0724	1.5709	2.0877	2.1385
		Put	−0.3832	−0.7854	−0.9167	−0.4718	−0.3762	−0.3560
	12	Call	−0.6524	−0.2054	1.6851	2.3628	3.9477	3.9365
		Put	−0.3984	−0.6293	−1.0045	−0.7535	−0.6877	−0.6841
CHF	**2**	**Call**	0.2176	0.0369	−0.1490	−0.0955	0.2542	0.3161
		Put	−0.0815	−0.0399	0.0065	−0.2127	−0.0615	−0.0700
	3	**Call**	−0.1031	−0.3889	−0.5900	−0.0181	0.4893	0.8593
		Put	−0.0291	−0.0836	−0.4601	−0.1044	−0.1542	−0.0927
	6	**Call**	−0.3809	−0.8497	0.0290	0.4156	1.2722	2.1344
		Put	−0.2463	−0.5273	−0.3569	−0.3670	−0.4229	−0.3723
	9	**Call**	0.3274	−0.4418	0.1648	2.0585	0.9817	1.1261
		Put	−0.2785	−0.3262	−0.2343	−0.6452	−0.6432	−0.5637
	12	**Call**	1.6239	−0.7295	−2.1261	2.5772	1.2260	1.4023
		Put	−0.1311	−0.3272	−0.8297	−0.6022	−0.8241	−0.7090
SEK	**2**	**Call**	0.0123	0.3461	1.4592	1.4886	1.1483	1.0335
		Put	−0.0098	−0.2084	−0.4421	−0.2134	−0.0841	−0.0592
	3	**Call**	0.7559	1.1395	1.7131	1.9035	1.6441	1.5500
		Put	−0.2957	−0.3093	−0.3084	−0.2717	−0.1344	−0.1022
	6	**Call**	0.9351	1.1749	1.0752	1.0267	0.9926	1.0701
		Put	−0.7596	−0.9341	−0.6787	−0.2776	−0.1799	−0.1784
	9	**Call**	0.8081	1.0251	1.7194	2.1410	1.8601	1.9745
		Put	−0.4823	−0.5175	−0.9438	−0.5530	−0.3628	−0.3600
	12	**Call**	0.4260	0.7763	0.8931	1.7251	1.9160	1.8374
		Put	−0.4796	−0.7661	−0.9821	−0.6574	−0.5749	−0.5876
JPY	**2**	**Call**	−1.5738	0.2209	2.0314	0.8080	−0.5993	−1.0159
		Put	0.1574	0.1400	0.3049	0.2075	−0.3306	−0.4356

Ccy	Std. maturity	Option	Moneyness					
			−0.1	−0.15	−0.35	0.35	0.15	0.1
	3	Call	−2.1189	0.2390	4.4618	1.6181	0.6417	0.6188
		Put	0.2552	0.2228	0.4417	0.4168	−0.1097	−0.3029
	6	Call	−5.7370	−1.3373	3.3992	1.0059	1.0598	1.4034
		Put	0.4826	0.4728	0.4695	0.5411	−0.0412	−0.2233
	9	Call	−5.7200	−2.2201	2.0625	−1.8468	−2.9837	−1.1671
		Put	1.2427	1.2582	0.6731	−0.6666	−1.5754	−0.8791
	12	Call	−3.2277	−1.0243	0.0171	−1.8888	−3.6459	−1.4965
		Put	0.6805	0.5591	−0.0209	−0.1584	−1.0924	−1.4079
CAD	1	Call	−0.0009	−0.0458	0.0107	0.4562	1.1845	1.7157
		Put	0.0552	0.0711	−0.0250	−0.1337	−0.1587	−0.1315
	3	Call	−0.1827	−0.0619	0.5819	1.2437	1.9510	2.3868
		Put	−0.0351	−0.2083	−0.3210	−0.3480	−0.2495	−0.2051
	6	Call	0.1614	0.3509	1.1714	0.8555	1.0527	1.3769
		Put	−0.2334	−0.3182	−0.8214	−0.4297	−0.3690	−0.3403
	9	Call	−0.1608	0.1862	0.6187	0.9127	0.7138	1.3908
		Put	−0.2830	−0.4549	−0.7047	−0.3085	−0.3094	−0.2966
	12	Call	−0.9650	−0.6925	−0.3443	−0.5226	−0.5630	0.1330
		Put	−0.3172	−0.6380	−0.9956	−0.1639	−0.2917	−0.2997
AUD	2	Call	−0.1279	0.0513	0.5684	0.6472	−0.0306	−0.0351
		Put	0.0758	−0.0268	−0.3280	−0.1852	−0.1151	−0.0889
	3	Call	0.2314	0.2788	0.6805	0.7822	0.0881	−0.0367
		Put	−0.1586	−0.1481	−0.2024	−0.1918	−0.1453	−0.1213
	6	Call	0.2143	0.5549	0.8018	0.2973	−0.7039	−0.9625
		Put	−0.1644	−0.3941	−0.5819	−0.1999	−0.0579	−0.0791
	9	Call	−0.0655	−0.1495	0.3957	0.3686	−1.7333	−3.3291
		Put	−0.0640	−0.1423	−0.6356	−0.3379	0.0461	−0.0487
	12	Call	−0.8863	−0.5713	−0.3788	−0.5221	−1.7522	−3.8909
		Put	−0.1404	−0.2399	−0.3753	−0.3670	0.0964	0.0699

Remark: There are 254 samples in each currency option combination. The critical value at the 95 percent confidence level is 1.96.

5.3.3 CNY analysis

Table 5.4 lists the t-statistics for all currency option combinations under the CNY test. The t-statistics of 15 out of 60 (25 percent) currency option groups are larger than the critical value 1.96, thus rejecting the null hypothesis that the average of VV replication errors is smaller than or equal to the average of the BS replication errors. In addition, the number of currency option groups that registered a negative t-statistic was reduced to 18 out 60 (30 percent). The results suggest that the Vanna-Volga method fails to dominate the Black-Scholes framework in terms of dynamic portfolio replication for the CNY.

Table 5.4 t-statistics for CNY test

Ccy	Std. maturity	Option	Moneyness					
			−0.1	*−0.15*	*−0.35*	*0.35*	*0.15*	*0.1*
CNY	2	**Call**	0.81477	1.58811	1.54891	0.40677	−0.66733	−1.64677
		Put	0.13987	0.14729	0.06117	0.18162	−0.15846	−0.36764
	3	**Call**	3.46048	3.80265	3.87532	1.82875	−1.55791	−4.73170
		Put	0.14378	0.12869	0.02211	0.33476	−0.62463	−0.79710
	6	**Call**	5.57534	5.75766	3.48160	2.49750	−3.61205	−7.08444
		Put	0.14225	0.18191	0.22704	0.44292	−0.06303	−0.96645
	9	**Call**	5.73911	5.84365	5.53136	2.92494	−4.59946	−14.19566
		Put	0.17605	0.21156	0.26037	0.35775	0.90528	−0.71025
	12	**Call**	5.36547	5.82694	5.14668	5.62349	−6.49689	−22.22886
		Put	0.24040	0.28487	0.32389	0.58736	1.18734	−1.26282

Remark: There are 504 samples in each cell. The critical value at the 95 percent confidence level is 1.96.

5.4 Conclusions

The empirical study demonstrates that the replication performance of a currency option with a major currency as underlying is improved when volatility is updated regularly in accordance with the quadratic approximation derived by the Vanna-Volga method. There is improvement in replication performance over the Black-Scholes model, in which the volatility is kept constant throughout the life of the currency option.

The error resulting from dynamic portfolio replication increases with a decreasing degree of moneyness. In other words, when the strike rate is close to the spot currency rate, the replication error tends to be smaller. When the strike rate is either materially below or above the spot currency rate, the replication error increases steadily. This observation is consistent with the results of volatility recovery as discussed in Chapter 3.

Similar improvement in replication performance is not observed for currency options with the CNY as the underlying currency. The result is explained by the fact that the currency rate for CNY does not follow the underlying theory of the development of the Vanna-Volga method.

6 Conclusions

In this book, we have assessed the Vanna-Volga method to determine whether it is superior to the Black-Scholes model for managing current options in financial institutions. On the basis of the implementation of the theories developed in Chapters 4, 5 and 6 and the empirical tests conducted with market data, the study provides a positive response to the questions set out in Chapter 1. These questions and the corresponding findings are summarized here.

- Is the Vanna-Volga method an accurate approach to valuate currency options?

Yes, the Vanna-Volga method is an accurate approach to valuing currency options. In particular, quadratic approximation facilitates the recovery of volatility with a high degree of accuracy with a closed-form solution. Using the Vanna-Volga method, the performance of the volatility recovery approaches deteriorates with decreasing degree of moneyness. When recovering a volatility smile, they work well for major currency in regular markets, moderately for major currency in stress markets and marginally for the CNY.

- How robust is the Vanna-Volga method in recovering a volatility smile?

Yes, the Vanna-Volga method is robust in recovering a volatility smile. Even though the volatility recovery approaches deteriorate with decreasing degree of moneyness, using quadratic approximation for major currencies under regular market conditions enables us to recover the volatilities at the extremities with an acceptable degree of accuracy

- Is the volatility smile derived from the Vanna-Volga method efficient in calculating the one-day VaR amount?

Yes, the volatility smile derived from the Vanna-Volga method is efficient in calculating the one-day VaR amount. Following the back testing methodology in the Basel II framework, in general, for major currencies, the volatility estimated by quadratic approximation will derive an accurate one-day VaR amount under regular market conditions. The exceptions are well explained by other factors that impact the accuracy of the one-day VaR amounts.

- Is the Vanna-Volga method effective in performing dynamic portfolio replication?

Yes, the performance of the Vanna-Volga method is superior to the Black-Scholes model for major currencies in dynamic portfolio replication. When the replicating portfolios are rebalanced on the days when left/right 25-Delta volatilities are readily available, the Vann-Volga method outperforms the Black-Scholes model for major currencies in terms of replication error.

In summary, Vanna-Volga method is superior to the Black-Scholes model for managing current options in financial institutions. For major currencies under regular market conditions, the Vanna-Volga method is easy to implement in closed-form solution with market data readily available from major financial information provider and is able to deliver volatility estimates and one-day VaR amounts with sufficient accuracy.

In contrast to its application to currency options with the seven major currencies as the underlying currency, the Vanna-Volga method does not produce any satisfactory results for the currency options with the CNY as underlying currency. This is explained by the fact that the CNY is under the Chinese government's foreign exchange control, which prevents the CNY from being freely traded in the international currency market. As such, the dynamics of the CNY are quite different from those of the other major currencies. This essentially opens an opportunity to study the currency options with the CNY underlying currency by applying other models. The continuous expansion of the CNY in the international finance warrants this effort.

In addition, the use of the Vanna-Volga method may be extended to the more complex structured currency products, for example the popular currency structured products "target accrual redemption forwards," which are synthesized by a series of currency options with different maturities and subject to a knockout accumulated profit target. This will broaden the application of the Vanna-Volga method.

References and further readings

Alexander, C. (2001). *Market Models: A Guide to Financial Data Analysis*. Chichester, West Sussex; New York: Wiley.

Alexander, C. (2009). *Market Risk Analysis*. Chichester, West Sussex; Hoboken, NJ: Wiley.

Ammann, M., and Buesser, R. (2013). Variance Risk Premiums in Foreign Exchange Markets. *Journal of Empirical Finance*, 23, 16–32.

Bank of East Asia. (2008). *Annual Report 2007*. Hong Kong: Bank of East Asia. http://www.hkbea.com/html/en/bea-about-bea-investor-communication-annual-and-interim-reports.html

Bank of East Asia. (2009). *Annual Report 2008*. Hong Kong: Bank of East Asia. http://www.hkbea.com/html/en/bea-about-bea-investor-communication-annual-and-interim-reports.html

Bank of East Asia. (2010). *Annual Report 2009*. Hong Kong: Bank of East Asia. http://www.hkbea.com/html/en/bea-about-bea-investor-communication-annual-and-interim-reports.html

Bank of East Asia. (2011). *Annual Report 2010*. Hong Kong: Bank of East Asia. http://www.hkbea.com/html/en/bea-about-bea-investor-communication-annual-and-interim-reports.html

Basel Committee on Banking Supervision (BCBS). (2009). *Revisions to the Basel II Market Risk Framework*. Bank for International Settlements. http://www.bis.org/bcbs/publications.htm?m=3%7C14%7C566.

Basel Committee on Banking Supervision (BCBS). (2011). *Interpretive Issues with Respect to the Revisions to the Market Risk Framework*. Bank for International Settlements. http://www.bis.org/bcbs/publications.htm?m=3%7C14%7C566.

Basel Committee on Banking Supervision (BCBS). (2011). *Revisions to the Basel II Market Risk Framework*. Bank for International Settlements. http://www.bis.org/bcbs/publications.htm?m=3%7C14%7C566.

Bank for International Settlements (BIS). (2010). *Triennial Central Bank Survey of Foreign Exchange and Derivatives Market Activity in 2010*. Bank for International Settlements. http://www.bis.org/list/bispapers/index.htm?m=5%7C27.

Bank for International Settlements (BIS). (2012). *OTC Derivatives Market Activity in the Second Half of 2011*. Bank for International Settlements. http://www.bis.org/list/bispapers/index.htm?m=5%7C27.

Basel Committee on Banking Supervision (BCBS). (2006). Basel II: International Convergence of Capital Measurement and Capital Standards: A Revised Framework - Comprehensive Version. Bank for International Settlements. http://www.bis.org/bcbs/publications.htm?m=3%7C14%7C566.

Beneder, R., and Elkenbracht-Huizing, M. (2003). Foreign Exchange Options and the Volatility Smile. *Medium Econometrische Toepassingen* 2.

Berkowitz, J., and O'Brien, J. (2002). How Accurate Are Value-at-Risk Models at Commercial Banks? *Journal of Finance*, 57(3), 1093–1111.

Bisesti, L., Castagna, A., and Mercurio, F. (2005). Consistent Pricing and Hedging of an FX Options Book. *Kyoto Economic Review*, 74(1), 65–83.

Black, F., and Sholes M. (1973). The Pricing of Options and Corporate Liabilities. *Journal of Political Economics*, 81(3), 637–645.

Bodie, Z., Kane, A. & Marcus, A. (2010). Investments (9th ed.). Boston, Massachusetts. McGraw-Hill Irwin.

Bossens, F., Rayée, G., Skantzos, N. S., and Deelstra, G. (2010). Vanna-Volga Methods Applied to FX Derivatives: From Theory to Market Practice. *International Journal of Theoretical and Applied Finance*, 13(8), 1293–1324.

Castagna, A. (2010). *FX Options and Smile Risk*. Chichester, West Sussex: Wiley.

Castagna, A., and Mercurio, F. (2006). Consistent Pricing of FX Options. Available at SSRN 873788.

Castagna, A., & Mercurio, F. (2007). Option Pricing: The Vanna-Volga Method for Implied Volatilities. *Risk*, 20(1), 106.

Clark, I. (2011). *Foreign Exchange Option Pricing*. Chichester, West Sussex: Wiley.

Corrado, C. J., & Su, T. (1996). S&P 500 Index Option Tests of Jarrow and Rudd's Approximate Option Valuation Formula. *Journal of Futures Markets*, 16(6), 611–629.

Creswell, J. (2009). *Research Design: Qualitative, Quantitative, and Mixed Methods Approaches* (3rd ed.). Thousand Oaks, CA: Sage.

Crouhy, M, Galai, D., & Mark, R. (2005). *Essentials of Risk Management*. Irwin: McGraw-Hill.

DeRosa, D. (2011). *Options on Foreign Exchange* (3rd ed.). Hoboken, New Jersey: Wiley.

Dowd, K. (2005). *Measuring Market Risk*. Chichester, West Sussex: Wiley.

Duan, J. C. (1995). The GARCH Option Pricing Mode. *Mathematical Finance*, 5(1), 13–32.

Fisher, T. (2007). *Variations on the Vanna-Volga Adjustment*. Bloomberg: Bloomberg Research Paper.

Forde, M. (2005). *Static Hedging of Barrier Options under the SABR Model and Local Volatility Model with Non-zero Interest Rates*. Doctoral dissertation, School of Mathematics, University of Bristol

Franke, J., Hardle, W. K., and Hafner, C. M. (2011). *Statistics of Financial Markets: An Introduction*. Berlin: Springer Science and Business Media.

Hair, J. F., Black, W. C., Babin, B. J., Andeson, R.E., and Tatham, R.L. (2006). *Multivariate Data Analysis*. Upper Saddle River, NJ: Pearson Prentice Hall.

Hang Seng Bank. (2008). *Annual Report 2007*. Hong Kong: Hang Seng Bank. https://bank.hangseng.com/1/2/about-us/investor-relations/financial-info/financial-statements.

Hang Seng Bank. (2009). *Annual Report 2008*. Hong Kong: Hang Seng Bank. https://bank.hangseng.com/1/2/about-us/investor-relations/financial-info/financial-statements.

Hang Seng Bank. (2010). *Annual Report 2009*. Hong Kong: Hang Seng Bank. https://bank.hangseng.com/1/2/about-us/investor-relations/financial-info/financial-statements.

Hang Seng Bank. (2011). *Annual Report 2010*. Hong Kong: Hang Seng Bank. https://bank.hangseng.com/1/2/about-us/investor-relations/financial-info/financial-statements.

Heston, S. (1993). A Closed-Form Solution for Options with Stochastic Volatility with Applications to Bond and Currency Options. *Review of Financial Studies*, 6(2), 327–343.

Hongkong and Shanghai Banking Corporation. (2008). *Annual Report 2007*. London: Hongkong and Shanghai Banking Corporation. http://www.hsbc.com/investor-relations/financial-and-regulatory-reports.

Hongkong and Shanghai Banking Corporation. (2009). *Annual Report 2008*. London: Hongkong and Shanghai Banking Corporation. http://www.hsbc.com/investor-relations/financial-and-regulatory-reports.

Hongkong and Shanghai Banking Corporation. (2010). *Annual Report 2009*. London: Hongkong and Shanghai Banking Corporation. http://www.hsbc.com/investor-relations/financial-and-regulatory-reports.

Hongkong and Shanghai Banking Corporation. (2011). *Annual Report 2010*. London: Hongkong and Shanghai Banking Corporation. http://www.hsbc.com/investor-relations/financial-and-regulatory-reports.

Hull, J. (2008). *Options, Futures, and Other Derivatives* (8th ed.). Upper Saddle River, NJ: Prentice Hall.

Hull, J., and White, A. (1998). Value-at-Risk When Daily Changes in Market Variables Are Not Normally Distributed. *Journal of Derivatives*, 5(3), 9–19.

J. P. Morgan. (1994). *RiskMetrics* – Technical Document (4th ed.). New York: Reuters.

Kupiec, P. (1995). Techniques for Verifying the Accuracy of Risk Management Models, Journal of Derivatives, 3, 1995, 73–84.

Kwok, Y., and Wong H. (2000). Currency-Translated Foreign Equity Options with Path-Dependent Features and Their Multi-asset Extensions. *International Journal of Theoretical and Applied Finan*ce, 3(2), 257–278.

Lam, K., Chang, E., and Lee M.C. (2002), An Empirical Test of the Variance Gamma Option Pricing Model. *Pacific-Basin Finance Journal*, 10(3), 267–285.

Lee, R. (2004). The Moment Formula for Implied Volatility at Extreme Strikes. *Mathematical Finance*, 14(3), 469–480.

Lopez, J. (1996). "Evaluating the Predictive Accuracy of Volatility Models, Research Paper #9524-R, Research and Market Analysis Group, Federal Reserve Bank of New York.

Madan, D., Carr, P., and Chang, E. (1998). The Variance Gamma Process and Option Pricing. *European Finance Review*, 2(1), 79–105.

Malz, A. (1997). Option-Implied Probability Distributions and Currency Excess Return. Federal Board of New York Staff Report No. 32.

Martin, W., and Bridgmon, K. (2012). *Quantitative and Statistical Research Methods*. San Francisco, California: Jossey-Bass.

Mercurio, F. (2002). *A Multi-stage Uncertain-Volatility Model*. Banca IMI Working Paper. http://www.fabiomercurio.it/UncertainVol.pdf

Mercurio, F. (2003). *Pricing and Static Replication of FX Quanto Options*. Banca IMI Internal Report. http://www.fabiomerucrio.it/fwdstartquanto.pdf.

Merton, R. (1973). Theory of Rational Option Pricing. *Bell Journal of Economics and Management Science*, 4(1), 141–183.

O'Kane, D. (2008). *Modelling Single Name and Multi-Name Credit Derivatives*. Chichester, West Sussex: Wiley.

Reiswich, D., and Wystup Uwe. (2009). FX Volatility Smile Construction. *Wilmott*, 2012(60), 58–69.

Sankaran, M. (1963). Approximations to the Non-central Chi-Squared Distribution. *Biometrika*, 50(1–2), 199–204.

Shkolnikov, Y. (2009). Generalized Vanna-Volga Method and Its Applications. Available at SSRN 1186383.

Wystup, U. (2008). *FX Options and Structured Products*. Chichester, West Sussex: Wiley.

Zikmund, W. G., Babin, B. J., Carr, J. C., and Griffin, M. (2010). *Business Research Methods*. Australia: South-Western Cengage Learning.

Index